WITHDRAWN

Detroit Cars

Fifty Years of the Motor City

Detroit Cars

Fifty Years of the Motor City

Martin Derrick

PRC

Produced in 1999 by
PRC Publishing Ltd,
Kiln House, 210 New Kings Road, London SW6 4NZ

This edition published 2001
Distributed in the U.S. and Canada by:
Sterling Publishing Co., Inc.
387 Park Avenue South
New York, NY 10016

ISBN 1-85648-587-0

Printed and bound in Hong Kong

Acknowledgements.

The author would like to thank first and foremost Nicky Wright, an Englishman living in Detroit, without whose unrivalled photography collection of American cars this book would not have been possible. Thanks as well to Anne Hope whose Motor Industry Archive also supplied pictures, and to Ford, General Motors and Chrysler press office staff in Detroit for information and photography.
Many thanks also to Sarah Tosh for her untiring assistance in organising pictures and captions.

Contents

Introduction

The auto industry touches all Americans in a way that no other industry does. As in so many things, the Americans were not first to build an auto, but once they got started they very quickly built the biggest and the best. They could afford to do this because during the 20th century America — the land of the free and the land of limitless opportunity for all — enjoyed an economy that was continually expanding, give or take the odd hiccup such as the 1929 Wall Street Crash and the later Great Depression. An expanding economy meant more money in people's pockets and the one thing they all dreamed of was owning an auto.

The auto industry, developing to satisfy this desire, actually changed the face of America in more ways than one. Not only did more cars mean more mobility, more roads, more travel, and yet more opportunities. But the industry itself, which gravitated to Detroit on the Great Lakes, required more and more workers to build its products. Detroit grew and migrant workers came from all over the USA to join in the 20th century gold rush that was the auto industry. In particular, Detroit

8

induced the biggest ever migration of southern state citizens to the north thanks to the promise of the highest wages available to both skilled and unskilled workers anywhere in America.

But the bedrock of the success of the US auto industry lies in the autos and trucks its produces. From the Ford Model T of the earliest days, through the great Chevies, GTOs, Corvettes, Mustangs, and Thunderbirds of the 1950s and 1960s, and right up to today's icons — perhaps the Dodge Viper, the Chrysler Voyager, and even the latest electronics-laden Lincoln Continental — the American people have always wanted autos to dream about, to aspire to, and, in their later years, autos whose histories were so vivid that they had the power to transport them back to their youth.

The Detroit auto industry is a world class business and one of the pillars of the massive American economy. But most important of all, it has always been and it remains today, the supreme icon of the great American dream. America as we know it today is the auto. And the auto is America.

Left: Henry Ford's production lines streamlined the mass manufacture of cars, and offered customers 'any color as long as it's black' in order to ensure that every car coming off the lines was identical — and therefore simpler and cheaper to manufacture.

Below: In the early days racing and speed trials were not only highly popular, but also the means by which fledgling auto-makers could prove the value of their engineering. Pictured is the Oldsmobile Pirate preparing for a speed run on the Florida sands in 1902.

Right: The world's first truly mass-produced car, the Ford Model T was a genuinely revolutionary product. It changed the American way of life by offering personal mobility at reasonable cost.

Far Right, Top: The Model T remained in production in various forms from 1908 to 1927, by which time over 14 million examples had been manufactured. Also built in the UK, it became a familiar sight on European roads.

Far Right, Bottom: Once the car became established, progress was remarkably quick in terms of both engineering and styling. Some of America's most elegant cars were produced in the pre-World War 2 years. Pictured is a 1935 Buick 8 Series 90.

Below: Another view of the Oldsmobile Pirate preparing for a speed run on the Florida sands in 1902.

The Birth of an Industry

America did not invent the motor car. Instead it invented the motor industry.

The news that the German company, Gottlieb Daimler, had succeeded in powering a horseless carriage with a four-cycle petrol engine in 1883 quickly crossed the Atlantic and then spread across the American continent like wildfire.

The idea of harnessing a power source to achieve self-propelled travel caught the imagination of hundreds, if not thousands, in America. Horseless carriages had been built before — Henry Ford himself was said to have caught the automotive bug when he saw a steam-powered vehicle huffing and puffing along the road as early as 1876 — but the key to success was recognized as being held by the Otto four-cycle engine, first developed by German Siegfried Marcus in 1873 and then refined by Nikolaus Otto in 1877.

The new technology even spawned its own magazine, *The Horseless Age*,

which reported in 1895 that more than 300 companies and American individuals were already at work trying to develop their own horseless carriages for the US market.

Among them were some destined to become household names: Henry Ford was working on a petrol-powered buggy from a rundown workshop in Detroit. It had a two-cylinder four-stroke engine driving the buggy through a lever and belt arrangement that gave the vehicle two forward speeds — 10mph or 20mph. Ford did not consider it necessary for his Quadricycle, as it was known, to incorporate either brakes or a reverse gear.

John and Horace Dodge were working in a Detroit machine shop, while Ransom Olds, having spent years trying to make a steam engine operate efficiently, had switched his attention to the petrol engine and would produce his first real car in 1896. David Buick was also working in Detroit; during the day he ran a plumbing business, but at night he was already working on ideas for making his own car. And Henry Leland was running a company involved in developing engines. His name doesn't appear on the front of any modern cars, but he was to become the founder of Cadillac.

However, in terms of the development of the American auto industry, it was another name that set the pace in the early days. Charles and Frank Duryea ran a bicycle business in Illinois but had ideas for a horseless carriage based on a farm wagon powered by a two-piston, one-cylinder, two-stroke petrol engine.

Above: Studebaker Champion. Studebaker was one of the few manufacturers who managed to produce a completely restyled car for 1946 when post-war car production was sanctioned. Novelties included wrap-around front windscreens on some models, shorter bonnets and longer boots. Stylistically this was taken to the extreme with the Champion coupe which, because its bonnet and boot were the same length, was known as the 'coming or going' Studebaker.

Above: Cadillac Derham Sedan. A minor styling revision for 1947 saw Cadillacs introduced with front grilles featuring five enormous horizontal bars. In other respects, they still retained pre-war styling and engineering.

It was left to Frank Duryea to develop the vehicle, to redesign the engine and to build a successful prototype. It was ready in time for a high-profile race in 1895 sponsored by the Chicago Times-Herald in order to raise interest in the horseless carriage which offered a winner's prize of $2,000 — a considerable sum in those days.

Run on Thanksgiving Day in a snowstorm, only six of the 100 entrants turned up and only two finished the 54-mile course. The winner was the Duryea, which crossed the line an hour and a half ahead of a Benz to claim the first prize at an average speed of 6.6mph.

At first glance, it was not much of a result. But in fact the race had an immense effect on the development of what was to become the American auto industry because of the interest it

generated among the public, among industrialists, and among the all-important investors.

The Duryea car itself also did more than merely win a race. Its success encouraged the brothers to move on to develop a new car for sale to the general public — the Duryea Motor Wagon. It continued to win races and one was even bought by the Barnum & Bailey circus for parading in its ring. But more important that these, the Duryea lays claim to being the very first volume-produced car in the world. They may have made only 13 examples before the Duryeas ran out of capital and were forced to sell their company, but they showed the way forward lay in the production of runs of identical vehicles.

Henry Ford was later to refine and develop the whole process of mass-production, but in the meantime, Detroit was to become the epicentre of the American car industry.

Why Detroit? Quite simply, because Ransom Olds, founder of the Oldsmobile company, set up his car factory in the city in 1899. He chose Detroit because it would be a good distribution center, being situated on the Great Lakes, and it also promised a good pool of relatively skilled labor.

His car, known as the Curved Dash, showed that mass-production of a small, relatively inexpensive, and simple car, could be an economic reality. Olds built 425 Curved Dash cars, each with a single cylinder engine producing seven horsepower and selling for $650.

More importantly, the suppliers he did business with, and the engineers he employed in and around Detroit, attracted others to the area. Quite simply, Detroit became the place to be for anyone wanting to get into the fast growing motor industry.

Of all those attracted to Detroit, it was Henry Ford who made the biggest early impression. Famous for introducing the production line to streamline the mass manufacture of cars, and for offering customers 'any color as long as it's black' in order to ensure that every car coming off the lines was identical — and therefore simpler and cheaper to manufacture — he actually started off his automotive career with no interest in selling to the public whatsoever.

What interested Ford was motor racing and speed. He reckoned the way to make his name and steal a march on his competitors was to build the fastest car in the world — one that would gain the most publicity.

He won a 10-mile race organized by the Detroit Drivers Club at Grosse Point, Michigan in October 1901, collecting $1,000 in winnings and attracting backers who supported his later effort to beat the 112mph speed record set by a New York Central Railroad locomotive on a run to Chicago in 1893.

Other backers of the Henry Ford Company by now wanted to see some tangible return on their investment and to see a production car being built and sold. Henry Leland, a famous manufacturer of precision parts was brought in to work on the production car, but inevitably he and Ford fell out, since

Ford was still directing all his energies into the development of the Ford Model 999 — a massive 1,153cu in racer with which he hoped to smash the speed record.

Ford resigned from the company that bore his name, taking away $900 and the blueprints of his race car. He also insisted that the company would no longer use his name. And so it was that a year later, when Henry Leland's car was launched, the company was renamed the Cadillac Automobile Company. Cadillac was to become one of the best known names in the American auto industry, but Ford too was to make his name before long.

He formed a new company, the Ford Motor Co, in 1903 and bought a small plant on Detroit's Mack Avenue to build a new car. He raised $28,000 in capital from 12 far-sighted investors, hired ten men, ordered 650 chassis from the Dodge brothers, and set to work.

The first 25 Model A cars, all identical with two-cylinder engines, were sold by July of that year at $850 each. By the end of the year, 1,708 had been sold and Ford had already made a profit approaching $100,000 in his first year of trading.

Next year, sales were up to 1,695 cars and the latest Model C had been launched. Ford also made an attempt on the land speed record that year, taking his Arrow racer to the frozen Lake St. Clair where a track was swept on the ice and then laid with cinders. Ford duly raised the record from 84mph to 91mph and in the process boosted sales of Ford cars beyond his wildest dreams. So great was the demand that just one year later, in 1905 — and still only two years after the company was formed — Ford was able to build a new factory on Piquette Avenue that was ten times larger than the Mack Avenue site.

The Arrival Of True Mass Production

America's auto industry pioneers thought differently to their European counterparts. In Europe, early cars were being built largely on coachmaking principles — each unit essentially hand-made and each part being machined to fit and to work in the engine or assembly for which it was intended.

By taking a different approach, the Americans were to leapfrog the Europeans into a technological lead that saw the US industry develop and grow at an awesome rate.

Most of the credit should probably go to Henry Leland's Cadillac company. He refused to accept that every transmission would have to be assembled by a skilled technician to ensure all the gears would mesh. He also refused to accept that pistons would need special machining to fit into bores that would probably also need honing to match the pistons.

Leland had started his career in a precision machining company and so he knew what was possible. And he insisted that all parts for his Cadillac cars had to be interchangeable — which, needless to say, meant that they had to be manufactured to exactly the same tolerances.

At first, no one believed it was possible but the doubters were silenced by a test undertaken by the Royal Automobile Club in England in 1908. They selected three Cadillac runabouts from the company's new London showroom and drove each 50 miles, much of it around the famous Brooklands race track.

They then stripped each car right down, reducing each to its 721 component parts. Club officials then randomly

Below: 1947 Ford Sportsman
Woody. For some years after
World War II ended, Ford,
like the other American
manufacturers, could do
little more than restyle what
were essentially 1942 or
even earlier models. A typical
example is the Sportsman
Woody, fitted with a V8 and
featuring the characteristic
wooden side treatment.

mixed up the components, producing three new piles of Cadillac parts. The three cars were then re-assembled, started and driven a further 500 miles at Brooklands at an average speed of some 34mph.

Leland and Cadillac had proved that interchangeability of parts was possible without adversely affecting either performance or reliability.

It was a massive breakthrough for the developing auto industry because now components suppliers could and would be given a specification and would be expected to produce parts to that exact specification and tolerance.

Once the car plants had a reliable source of identical parts at their disposal, it took just one more leap of faith to really set the industry moving.

That leap was made by Henry Ford with the launch off the Model T in 1908. Ford had already promised that he would build a car for the masses, large enough to be practical for a family, but compact enough to be run by an individual. It would be constructed of the best available materials and use the very latest technology, but it would also be priced so that any man on a good salary could afford to own one, and, as he put it, to 'enjoy with his family the blessings of hours of pleasure in God's great open spaces.'

The Model T was an instant success, attracting 1,000 enquiries the day it was launched in October 1908 at a price of $850. When it was introduced, Ford produced about 10% of America's cars, but so great was the response to the new Model T that by 1914, Ford's market share was over 50%.

The Model T was a ground-breaking design in many ways. For example, it featured a separate cylinder head for the first time, as Ford had discovered that slicing the top off the block made it easier to machine. It also employed new

lightweight materials such as vanadium steel. It had two sets of brakes, a water-cooled four-cylinder engine, and even a magneto built into the flywheel. The Model T was light, durable, simple to maintain and operate, and inexpensive to own.

But the most revolutionary aspect of the Model T was the way in which it was made. Like Cadillac, Ford insisted on parts that were precisely manufactured so they could be fitted to any car. But Ford's breakthrough was in the introduction of a moving production line. It came not at the Model T's introduction, but a little later in 1913 when 29 men were positioned side by side alongside a long table to build magnetos. Instead of each building a complete unit, ten men were each allocated a single task and, having finished it, slid the entire unit along to the next man who then did his job. The bottom line was that whereas it took one man 20 minutes to build a complete magneto — and therefore 29 men 20 minutes to build 29 — using this new system, the assembly time fell to 13 minutes per unit. Later,

when the magneto units were moved along the table by a chain mechanism, production time fell to five minutes.

Ford enthusiastically adapted this production technology first to make engines and transmissions, then other sub-assemblies, and eventually the whole car.

In 1913, it took on average 12.5 hours to build a chassis. By fixing the chassis to a rope and moving it via a windlass, six assemblers moving with the chassis installing parts as they went, the job could be finished in under six hours. Next year, Ford introduced an endless chain to move the chassis along the production line and assembly time fell to 93 man-minutes per unit.

Mass production, with the lower costs, greater reliability, and high quality that went with it, had come of age. And it had an immediate effect on costs: in 1912, the price of a Model T touring car had already come down from the initial $850 to $600. By 1916 the price was down to $360, and Ford was enjoying annual sales of $100 million.

Above: Buick Super 9 Sedan. Post-war, Buick hoped to emulate its pre-war success story with the Buick Super which was based on modern styling and first-rate engineering that produced a middle class status symbol that offered a lot of car for the money.

The Growth Years

The first half of the 20th century was one of massive growth for America's auto industry. As the wealth of the country increased, so the demand for cars continued to grow. And ironically, the motor industry itself provided much of that economic growth and in turn much of the demand for its own products.

Ford, for example, was paying its workers $5 a day as early as 1914 — about double the current rate for unskilled labor. Women were excluded from this bonanza, as Henry Ford reckoned their task was to go off and get married; and men too could lose out if Ford's Sociological Department spies discovered any signs of bad living — which included gambling, having an unkept house or yard, and even not taking enough baths.

The wages, however, were sufficient to start a move of people and labor from the southern states to Detroit in search of work and the sort of income that blue collar workers could only dream of elsewhere.

As early as 1913, General Motors had introduced finance packages that would allow a $500 car to be driven away for a down payment of around $125. Needless to say, it was not the

notoriously conservative banking industry that was leading this early foray into consumer credit. But so great was the demand for cars that by 1924 it is estimated that 75% of new cars were already being bought on credit.

The financing of autos started a revolution in America — a fundamental change in outlook that swept aside earlier values such as thrift and savings to one of consumerism. Consumers now drove the American economy to support mass production and high blue collar wages; and in turn, those consumers were supported by the availability of easy credit.

As more Americans bought autos, so more was spent on repairing and maintaining them, on developing the road system and on building gas stations. Growth in demand for autos meant growth in demand for petrol and in the early days, that meant an improvement in the environment — a supreme irony.

Back in 1901, near Beaumont, Texas, a gusher of oil some 200ft high crashed out of an exploratory drilling pipe. This was the massive Spindletop oil find which was to start an oil bonanza that produced more wealth than even the California Gold Rush of 1848 and 1849.

With the spindletop geyser producing up to 100,000 barrels of oil a day, the speculators rushed to Texas and

Above: Packard Super Deluxe. Packard appealed above all to the growing middle classes in America. Their advertising suggested the cars were easily affordable for those on middle incomes, but the downside of this publicity approach was that the Packard name tended to lose some of its exclusivity.

transformed Beaumont into a boom town almost overnight. Less than a year after the initial find, there were already 214 wells on the same hill, all seeking a share of the black gold.

At that time, there was strong demand for fuel oil, used by factories, ships and railroads, and also for kerosene, used in the homes of rural America, as well as lubricating oils and greases. However, there was little demand for gasoline, a by-product of the oil refining process that the oil companies found difficult to deal with, or to find a use for. So, in the main, they simply poured it into nearby rivers and streams, causing untold damage to waterlife, plants, and the environment generally.

But with the growth in demand for automobiles, salvation was at hand. Better still, the development of the oil industry was taking place at exactly the same time that mass-production was being introduced in Detroit. The auto industry needed the oil industry and the oil industry needed the auto industry. And so the Texas oil find was yet another reason why the American auto

industry was able to grow so quickly in comparison with its European rivals over the Atlantic.

In the years running up to World War II, that growth was phenomenal. Just before auto production ceased in 1941, Detroit was producing 3,731,000 cars per annum. Automatic transmission, air conditioning, and dashboard radios were already commonplace.

During the war, the Detroit factories were turned over to military production, and their achievements are astonishing: General Motors produced 13,000 bombers and another 200,000 aircraft engines, 38,000 armored vehicles, 854,000 trucks, 90,000 artillery guns and nearly two million machine

guns. Ford built 8,685 B-24 Liberator bombers, another 58,000 aircraft engines, 2,700 tanks, 12,400 armored cars, over 93,000 trucks and 278,000 Jeeps. Chrysler, Packard, Studebaker, and Nash-Kelvinator were all involved in the war effort too, with the result that when peacetime auto production could start again, the factories were all in good shape.

In 1946, 1.8 million cars were built and just three years later, production topped four million units. The six million milestone came in 1950, seven million in 1955 and the magic ten million mark was reached in 1972.

Above: The Cadillac Series 62 Sedan was the first Cadillac to go into production in the post-war period. It was based on the General Motor's C-Body, which had also been used in Buicks and Oldsmobiles. The Series 62, however, was easily identified by its racy-looking notchback top.

Above: The Kaizer-Fraser company was set up in 1945 with the intention of building inexpensive front-wheel drive Kaiser cars in California and more expensive Frazer cars in Detroit. In the end, the front-wheel drive idea was dropped and both Kaizer and Frazer were broadly similar in engineering terms.

Right: Hudson Commodore. Hudson's post-war design was so low that it became known as the 'step-down' Hudson. Just 60in high — six or seven inches lower than most of its competitors — the Hudson's advertisements of the time boasted it was the '4-most' car of its time, giving four reasons:
• the most beautiful
• the most roomy
• the most road-worthy
• the most all-round performance model.

Left: Willys Jeepster. After the war, Willys sought ways of breaking into the mass car market by extending its existing Jeep range. One effort was the Jeepster, fitted with both four- and six-cylinder engines and featuring a mechanically operated soft top.

Below: Chrysler Town and Country Convertible Sedan. 1948's Chrysler Town and Country series adopted the unique wood bodied line for the four door sedan and for the convertible. A trial quantity of hardtops were built using the convertible's body.

Above: Pontiac Silver Streak. Pontiac's post-war models were distinguished by the company's 'Silver Streak' styling consisting of bands of chrome along the top of the hood. Front grilles were also styled with increasing quantities of chrome horizontal bars.

Left: Cadillac Series 61 Sedanette. The big news at Cadillac in 1949 was the launch of a new overhead valve V8 engine. Consequently there were only minor changes to the cars' appearances. The Cadillac's Series 61 range was still without front fender shields and panel moldings.

Above: Cadillac Coupe DeVille. Top of the Cadillac range, the pillarless two-door Coupe DeVille cost $3,496 in 1949. Under its lengthy hood was a new 331cu in overhead valve V8 producing 160hp.

Right: The small Crosleys with their 26.5bhp 44cu in four-cylinder engines, were very successful in the immediate post-war years. Most popular of the bodystyles were station wagons, but problems, including a tendency for the the engines to lose all their cooling water, contributed to sales dropping off from 1949.

Above: The Frazer Manhattan was an upscale model introduced in 1948. Initially sold only as a four-door sedan, a convertible was launched in 1949.

Left: Cadillac Coupe DeVille.

Right: The Chrysler Windsor series was an updated version of the Royal. Fluid drive and Prestomatic transmission were standard on all models, as were padded dashboards for safety.

Below Right: Ford Convertible. The first all-new Ford cars since the war were launched in 1949. They included both standard Ford series and the upscale Custom series. Convertibles were only offered in the Custom Six and Custom V8 series.

Far Right: Cadillac Fastback. Cadillacs continued to offer a heady combination of both engineering excellence and attractive styling. The fastback in particular suggested a car capable of high performance.

The 1950s

With more than half America's cars over 10 years old, the start of the 1950s was a time of enormous demand. When production restarted in 1946, there were no truly new autos; immediate post-war cars were pre-war designs with maybe a new grille or some extra chromework.

But it did not take long for Detroit to get up and running after the war. The 1950s was a decade in which anything seemed possible. In terms of technology, leading engineers were already contemplating both jet-powered and even atomic cars. When Rover in England produced its gas-turbine prototype,

some revolutionary form of new power plant seemed inevitable and both Chrysler and General Motors quickly tested the gas turbine concept too.

Most of all, however, the 1950s was the decade of the most extravagant and outrageous styling. The fins, the chrome, the portholes, and the wild colors that characterize the American car of the time were first seen on another of the decade's innovations — the concept or dream car.

Nash-Kelvinator started the ball rolling in 1950 with its NX1 concept and soon all the major players got in on the act. The dream cars started the tradition — still going strong today — of concepts that have two purposes: to attract crowds and interest at Motor Shows and to give the public a glimpse of what the future may hold; and to allow engineers and designers to explore the edges of the technological and visual envelopes.

They also gave the manufacturers an opportunity to gauge public response

Above: 1950 Hudson Commodore Sedan. Hudson's first truly new post-war look was the 'step-down' design first introduced in 1947. Hudson Commodore models were the top line versions featuring more luxurious interior trim, but sharing six- and eight-cylinder engines with the Hudson Super models.

and therefore gear their future production plans to customer demand.

But the decade also brought a plethora of exciting new production cars, including the plastic-bodied Corvette, its competitor from Ford, the Thunderbird, the upmarket Lincoln Mk IV, the Studebaker Hawk, the ill-fated Ford Edsel, and the rather more successful Eldorado and Continental.

In terms of power plants, it was also the decade in which the V8 became the staple engine in the USA. Chrysler introduced its famous 'Hemi' V8, while both Ford and GM made V8s virtually standard on all models other than the very cheapest which retained straight sixes.

In terms of power output, the race was on and by the end of the decade, Ford's 352cu in V8 was producing

300bhp, Plymouth's 350cu in was producing 315bhp and Chrysler's Hemi was bored out to 354cu in for the New Yorker model which boasted 340bhp. Cadillac's 365cu in V8 reached the magical 365bhp but there was yet more to come: Chrysler's 300H model was producing a massive 405bhp in 1962 before the Detroit manufacturers turned their attention away from sheer brute power.

In 1950 there were still some 40 American car makers, though 19 marques were already owned by the Big Three in Detroit. During the decade, Nash merged with Hudson to form American Motors, Packard merged with Studebaker and Kaizer took over Willys-Overland. None of the new and larger companies lasted long and even the strongest, American Motors, was eventually taken over by Chrysler.

Above: 1950 Hudson Commodore 8 Convertible. Hudson production was resumed in Canada in 1950, the year in which the Commodore Convertible was introduced. Hydraulic windows and leather trim were standard, while a 'fold-away' rear window was optional.

Right: 1950 Nash Air Flight Convertible. Nash's interesting post-war design, the Airflyte, had a smooth fastback style at the rear and both front and rear wheels partially enclosed. Critics dubbed it 'the bathtub' but its unitary construction was an indication of its high-quality engineering.

Below: 1950 Ford Custom Convertible. First introduced in 1949, Ford's first all-new cars since the war showed self-confident styling, including the word 'FORD' boldly mounted above the grille in capital letters. Six- and eight-cylinder versions producing 95hp and 100hp respectively were offered with either three-speed manual transmission or three-speed with automatic overdrive.

Above: 1950 Pontiac Silver Streak 8 Convertible. Trim changes were the most noticeable alterations to Pontiacs in 1950. Deluxes were given as much chrome as owners could polish, and an '8' was added between the words Silver Streak on the fenders of this model.

Left: 1950 Chevrolet Bel Air Hardtop. The most important news from the Chevrolet camp in 1950 was the addition of the sporty Bel Air hardtop. There was also the possibility of having fully automatic Powerglide transmission, which helped sales reach their highest point ever.

Right: 1950 Studebaker Champion Regal Deluxe. Early 1950s Studebakers could never be mistaken on the road thanks to their unique bullet nose styling. For 1950, the Champion Regal Deluxe gained a second chrome ring at the front and its straight six engine was revised to increase the power output to 85hp.

Below: 1950 Mercury Four-door Sedan. As early as the beginning of the 1950s Mercurys were becoming popular with the hot-rodding fraternity, and James Dean's choice of an early 1950s Mercury as his transport in the cult film *Rebel Without A Cause* helped sustain the Mercury's appeal to the young.

Above: 1950 Hudson Commodore Eights were fitted with an in-line eight-cylinder flathead engine producing 128hp. Four-door sedan, two-door coupe, two-door Hollywood, and two-door convertible models were available.

Left: 1951 Frazer Manhattan Convertible. Early Frazers were noted for their broad seats, generous interior space, and also their smooth lines. The established US auto industry had difficulty believing that Henry Kaiser — a sand, gravel, and ship-building entrepreneur — and Joseph Frazer — hitherto a GM auto salesman — could succeed as auto manufacturers, but they thrived at first.

Right: 1951 Oldsmobile 88. 1951 was the Oldsmobile 88's third year in production and it was proving to be a huge hit. Body and chassis were similar to the 76 series, but the 88's design had a lot more panache. Station wagons, however, had not done so well and Oldsmobile had halted production in 1950.

Below: 1951 Buick Super 8. Buick's Specials had smaller bodies than the Supers, but both were essentially very similar in appearance. The '8' of the Super's title referred to its eight-cylinder engine.

Above: Ford Custom Convertible. Extra chrome on the window moldings, horn ring, and the side of the body were added to the 1951 Ford Custom range — Ford's top trim level at the time. Of that year's total production of over 740,000 Customs, some 41,000 were the elegant convertible models.

Left: 1951 Desoto Custom Four-door Sedan. Not the most elegant cars on the road, DeSoto nevertheless managed to appeal to the middle-income car buyer. Based largely on Chrysler's mainstream designs, the Custom series was available as a sedan, coupe, convertible or station wagon.

Right: 1951 Ford Crestliner.
Ford's range was extended in
1951 to include the
Crestliner, a two-door sedan
with extra chrome and a
vinyl roof, the Victoria two-
door pillarless coupe, a convertible, and a Country
Squire two-door station
wagon. Prices then ranged
from $1,417 for a six-cylinder
two-door sedan to $2,110
for the V8 station wagon

Below: 1952 All State A230.
The 1952 All State was Sears
Roebuck's second effort at
selling an own-brand model.
Built for the retail company
by Kaiser-Frazer, it was simply
a Henry J model with a
different grille and Sears
Roebuck's own brand tyres
and battery

Above: 1952 Nash Healey. The Healey was developed as a result of a chance meeting on a trans-Atlantic liner between English sports car manufacturer Donald Healey and George Mason of Nash. Just over 500 examples were built in all.

Left: 1952 Packard Mayfair. Packard had earned a pre-war reputation for the finest quality engineering and coachbuilding — in fact Packard was often compared to Rolls-Royce in England. During the 1950s it never regained its position as America's leading prestige auto maker and despite some elegant efforts — such as the Mayfair model — the name would disappear in 1958.

Above: 1953 Buick Skylark. Buick's Roadmaster Skylark Convertible, introduced in 1953, was based on the standard Roadmaster and shared its 188bhp 322cu in V8 engine. However, it had newly designed fenders without Ventiports, a lowered roof line and unique 40-spoke wire wheels. The interior was leather, as befitted the top of the range.

Right: 1953 Oldsmobile Fiesta. In 1953, the luxury Oldsmobile, the Ninety Eight series, got even better. The limited edition Ninety Eight series Fiesta was brought out, giving customers a taste of the stylistic direction Olds was about to take.

Left: 1953 Kaiser Darrin. An elegant little two-door open topped roadster, the Kaiser Darrin was initially powered by a 161cu in straight six engine producing 90hp, though later 140hp V8s were offered. Fibreglass bodywork ensured the Darrin's weight was kept down and so the car was capable of both 100mph performance and 30mpg economy.

Below: 1953 Hudson Commodore. Commodore models of the early 1950s could be ordered with 127hp straight six or 128hp V8 engines. However, 'High-Output' engine options were also available, including a high compression version of the six and a 'Power Dome' version of the V8.

Right: 1953 Hudson Hornet. In its standard 1953 guise the Hornet was fitted with a range of straight six engines producing up to 145hp. However, a special X-7 engine producing around 200hp was available for racing and as a result Hudsons were able to win 22 of that season's 37 NASCAR races.

Below: 1953 Hudson Jet. Launched in 1953, the Jet was a downsized Hudson with slab-sided styling and a false air scoop on the hood to suggest higher power and performance than it could actually deliver.

Above: 1953 Ford Victoria. To meet customer demand, an all-new range of options was offered in 1952-53, to include radios, electric clocks, illuminated vanity mirrors, and a Magic Air heater. In addition, power steering, power brakes, white wall tyres, and tinted glass were all available at extra cost on this Crestline Victoria Hardtop.

Left: 1953 Studebaker Champion. With its 170cu. in. straight six producing a relatively modest 85hp, the Studebaker Champion was never going to be the quickest auto on the block. But its style still managed to set it apart from the crowd.

Above: 1953 Cadillac Series 62 Convertible. Since 1951, Cadillac had decided the Series 62 bodies would be five inches shorter than those of other ranges. Other identifying features included non-louvered rear fenders and the Cadillac crest on the hood and deck lid.

Right: 1953 Kaiser Dragon. Never able to match the supreme elegance of the Kaiser Derrin — described by Mrs Kaiser as the most beautiful car she had ever seen — the Kaiser Dragon nevertheless retained a certain unique style, including its strange roof line.

Left: 1953 Studebaker Commander. As life became increasingly difficult for the independents, Packard and Studebaker joined forces in 1954 to form the Studebaker-Packard Corporation. Studebaker continued to produce some elegant designs, including the Commander hardtop coupe, but the writing was already on the wall.

Below: 1954 Cadillac Eldorado. The luxury Eldorado convertible had been added to the Cadillac DeVille range in 1953. It had a full range of DeLuxe accessories, and a wraparound windshield: It looked more like a sports car than a luxury rag-top, and had been derived from Motorama's exhibition of futuristic dream machines.

Right: 1954 Buick Super Convertible. Buick's style had changed, with a less aggressive grille in 1953. Special models had retained the trusty straight eight-cylinder engine but Super and Roadmaster models were by now fitted with a new V8 which boosted output to 164hp.

Below Right 1954 Packard Caribbean. Aimed squarely at the luxury market, the Caribbean went into limited production in 195 , available as a convertible or a hardtop. For that princely sum, 400 owners enjoyed full leather upholstery, chrome wire wheels and a host of features such as power steering, a modern radio with twin electric aerials and electric windows.

Far Right, Top: 1954 Lincoln Capri Panamerican. Part of the Lincoln-Mercury division of Ford since 1945, Lincoln became a separate division in 1955 and immediately set about restyling its Capri series. Both hardtop Sport Coupe and four-door sedan derivatives were offered, both powered by Lincoln's 368cu in 285hp V8. This example was chosen to enter the rugged Panamerica race.

Far Right, Bottom: 1954 Ford Crestline. The Crestline remained Ford's top trim level in 1954. One of three new models introduced during 1954 was the Ford Crestline Sunliner, the convertible version. Also new was the Skyliner, a two-door pillarless coupe featuring a green tinted plastic insert over the front seats.

Right: 1954 Chevrolet Bel Air. The new 1954 Bel Air still had full genuine carpeting on its list of extra features, along with newly designed wheel disks. Bel Air was written between the double moldings on the rear fenders, along with the Chevrolet crest.

Below: 1954 Studebaker Commander. Even after Studebaker's trademark bullet nose styling was dropped, the company still managed to ensure its cars retained a distinctive Studebaker style. The Champion continued to attract buyers and keep the company afloat in difficult trading conditions.

Above: 1955 Dodge Royal Lancer. The Royal series was added to the top of the Dodge line-up in 1954. They had all the features of a Coronet, and a bit more chrome. The Royal 500 was a replica of the car that had paced the Indy 500 that year. The pace cars had dual exhausts and four-barrel carburetors.

Left: 1955 Chrysler 300B. Chrysler's 300 series enjoyed the distinction of being America's most powerful car in 1955. Its performance and styling marked it out from the crowd and ensured it would have enduring popularity.

Above: 1955 Chrysler C-300. The lowered Chrysler 300, introduced during 1955, was powered by a revised 331cu in V8 whose power was boosted to 300hp thanks to racing camshafts and twin exhausts and a pair of massive four-jet carburetors. Top speed was some 130mph.

Right: 1955 Chevrolet Bel Air. The Bel Air was Chevrolet's top series. By 1955, it had most of the features included on other, lower-priced lines, as well as carpets on closed body styles and a smarter line in upholstery fabrics. The Bel Air script was now gold and behind slanting vertical slash molding.

Left: 1955 Chevrolet Nomad. The Milestone two-door Chevrolet Nomad station wagon was part of the exclusive Bel Air series. It featured a unique two-door hardtop roof but overall was unlikely to win any automotive beauty contests.

Below: The two-door 1955 Ford Ranch Wagon was the company's cheapest station wagon in 1955, at $2,043 for six-cylinder models or $2,143 for the V8 alternative. The Country Wagon was the intermediate line, while the Country Squire was the top trim-level wagon at the time.

Right: 1955 Ford Fairline Sunliner. The Sunliner looked good but also performed well as Ford joined the horsepower race in 1955. Larger overhead-valve engines were introduced, producing up to 182hp in 'Power Pack' versions.

Below: 1955 Ford Fairline. The Fairlane range was totally restyled for 1955 with longer, lower, and wider bodies giving a sleeker appearance all-round. Pictured is the Skyliner two-door sedan.

Above: 1956 Mercury Monterey. With its deeply hooded headlights and front bumpers integrated with its grille, the Mercury Monterey sold over 100,000 units in 1956.

Left: 1956 Chevrolet Bel Air Two-door Hardtop. The Bel Air put the luxury into Luxury Line. Chrome wheel covers and chrome trim around the windows made sure it stood out from the crowd. In 1956, all Chevrolets with V8 engines had large V-shaped emblems place below the Chevrolet crest on the hood and on the deck.

Above: 1956 Buick Century. The Century name had been revived in 1954 for the first time since 1942. The car shared its body and running gear with the Special but featured the more powerful Roadmaster engine. At the time, this was Buick's performance car, producing a heady 195hp from its 322cu in V8.

Right: 1956 Nash Ambassador. Available as a four-door sedan or two-door hardtop coupe, the 1956 Nash Ambassador shared the styling of the Statesman model but was seven inches longer. On Custom models, Packard's 352cu in. V8 and Ultramatic transmission were under the hood.

Above: 1956 Packard
Executive. Packard suffered
severe problems with the
quality levels being achieved
at its body plant, and the
result was falling sales during
1956, despite the fact that
models such as the Packard
Executive offered unrivaled
performance for the price.

Left: 1956 Packard Clipper.
With its 289cu in 275hp V8,
the Packard Clipper four-
door sedan provided out-
standing performance levels
but sales of the marque
started slipping because of
fears about build quality.

Right: 1956 Ford Sunliner. An aggressive front grille and bright two-tone paintwork ensured the 1956 Ford Sunliner was never short of attention. At this time, white wall tires were requested by some 80% of buyers.

Below: 1956 Desoto Fireflite Convertible. By 1956, Desoto styling incorporated Chrysler's Forward Look, with longer and lower bodies and a wraparound windscreen. All models were by now powered exclusively by the Hemi V8, with Firedome versions producing 185hp and the top line Fireflight versions pushing out 200hp thanks to the adoption of a four-barrel Carter carburetor.

Above: 1956 Packard 400. Packard's 400 hardtop coupe was fitted with a brand new 352cu in V8 producing 260hp. To match the performance potential, the car was also fitted with revolutionary self-leveling suspension and an uprated Ultramatic automatic transmission.

Left: 1956 Cadillac Coupe DeVille. Sales records had peaked for Cadillac in 1955. The cars were still being marketed at the luxury end of the market, with features like automatic transmission and power brakes standard on all models. The Coupe DeVille stood out with its golden script nameplate

Above: 1956 Nash Metropolitan Convertible. The British-built Nash Metropolitan was available either in two-door coupe or two-door convertible versions. Power — such as it was at 42hp — derived from a mere 74cu in in-line four-cylinder engine. Yet the Metropolitan was a big hit because of its cheeky style and inexpensive running costs.

Right: 1956 Olds Super 88 Convertible Coupe. For 1956, the Oldsmobile 88 series cars were given a facelift that introduced a swept flank to get away from the boxy look that had previously characterized the model.

Left: 1956 Chrysler 300B. In 1956, Chrysler's 300B echoed the uniqueness of the first letter cars, introduced the previous year. Technically, the 300B was a subseries of the New Yorker. It came with two high performance hemi engines mated to either a manual or automatic transmission.

Below: 1957 Chevrolet Bel Air. Elegant and purposeful, the Chevrolet Bel Air introduced in 1957 was also extremely powerful, producing a magic 283hp from its 283cu in of displacement. Bel Airs were available in seven different bodystyles including sedans, hardtops, convertibles, and station wagons.

Right: 1957 Dual Ghia Firebomb. Bodies of the Chrysler Dual Ghia were hand-built in Italy by Ghia and then 318cu in Hemi V8s were installed at the Dual Motors plant in Detroit. The elegant Dual Ghia was built only between 1995 and 1957.

Below Right: 1957 Ford Fairlane Skyliner Retractable Hardtop. The Fairlane 500, Ford's flagship, was lower and longer than ever before and sported the latest styling craze — tailfins. While the Sunliner convertible was a conventional soft top, Ford also offered the Skyliner, advertised as the world's only hardtop convertible, whose roof folded into the boot at the touch of a button.

Below: 1957 Buick Century. Restyled bodywork that was longer and lower then ever before was the trademark of the 1957 Buick Century. With 300bhp on tap, the Century was the fastest model in Buick's range, and so sported four portholes in front of the doors instead of the three with which lesser models were endowed.

Left: 1957 Cadillac Sedan DeVille. 1957 was marked for Cadillac by the combination of brand new styling and technology it was now able to produce. The Series 62 had a new tubular X-frame which produced a lower body without cramping the interior. All models had the customary 'shark' style fins, of course.

Below Left: 1957 Lincoln Continental Mk II. The Continental Mark II was launched at the Paris Auto Show in October 1955, featuring a long hood and short rear trunk. It also displayed far less chrome than most of its contemporaries and perhaps this was part of the reason that it came to be considered one of the most beautiful of all American cars of its day.

Below: 1957 Hudson Hornet. The last Hudsons before the demise of the marque were launched in October 1957, two inches lower than before and sitting on new 14in wheels. The Hudson Hornet four-door sedan was fitted with a 255hp 327cu in V8 and a new Hydramatic automatic transmission but sales that year struggled to reach the 3,000 mark and AMC decided to drop the both the Hudson and Nash names to concentrate in future on the Rambler marque.

Right: 1957 Oldsmobile 88. To celebrate Old's 50th anniversary, the 88 entry series was renamed the Golden Rocket in 1957. Three-piece rear windows had been reintroduced and, for the first time in seven years, a station wagon was available.

Below Right: 1957 Ford Thunderbird. Restyled for 1957 to incorporate rear tailfins, the Thunderbird's longer boot also increased storage space. Though the standard 312cu in V8 now produced 245hp, a special engine could be ordered producing 270hp. If that was still insufficient power, a 300hp supercharged V8 was also available — a slightly toned-down version of the 340hp units used in NASCAR racing.

Below: 1957 Packard Clipper. Packard President James Nance had resigned in 1956 and Studebaker-Packard was acquired by the Curtiss-Wright Corporation. From that time, Packards such as the 1957 Clipper were based on Studebaker designs, but this was not what Packard customers wanted and sales slumped despite the fact that the Clipper was a very good all-round performer.

Left: 1957 Ford Fairline two-door sedan. Ford Fairlane models sat on a longer wheelbase than the entry Custom series and were also some five inches lower than before. Also noteable are the Fairlane's rear fins, which the company described at the time as 'high canted fenders'.

Below Left: 1957 Cadillac Eldorado Brougham. Launched in 1957, the Cadillac Eldorado Brougham was available in two-door coupe and four-door sedan versions — the latter having the distinction of being the first pillarless offered in America. The car, which featured every conceivable extra including cigarette, tissue and perfume dispensers, was made for only two years with total production of just over 700 examples.

Below: 1957 Lincoln Premiere. Additional head-lights and tail-lights enclosed in the rear fins were the chief styling changes on the 1957 Lincoln Premiere. The car was identical to the Lincoln Capri except for a different nameplate and a star medal-lion on the front fenders.

Above: 1957 Lincoln Premiere. All versions of the Premiere — including the smart convertible — were fitted with a 368cu in V8 producing 300hp which Lincoln promoted in its advertising as a positive safety feature.

Right: 1957 Chrysler New Yorker. The New Yorker was Chrysler's top range and in 1957 it had the biggest production car engine available. Displacement had been upped 10% to 392cu in and this in turn boosted output to 325hp. A dart strip livened up the sides of the New Yorker.

Above: 1957 Mercury Turnpike Cruiser. Fitted with more gadgets and gizmos than any other contemporary car, the Mercury Turnpike Cruiser boasted among its numerous standard fitments a retractable rear window, power seats and sliding door locks.

Left: 1957 Desoto Adventurer. The 1957 Adventurer deserves a foot-note in automotive history in that it was the very first standard US car whose horsepower equaled its engine displacement. The Adventurer, which produced 345hp from 345cu in, was not the first car to achieve this feat — both Chrysler and Chevrolet had similar models in 1956 and 1957 respectively — but their's achieved it with upgraded engines.

Right: 1957 Imperial Crown Convertible. Perhaps the most extravagently styled Imperial of them all, the 1957 model caught the mood of the times and contributed to the best ever sales year for Imperial. Power came from a 392cu in V8 producing 325hp, and a Torqueflite automatic transmission with push-button shift control was standard.

Below: 1957 Olds 98. 1957 was a good year for Oldsmobile. They had moved into fifth position in the league of best selling automakers with 6.2% of the market share. 'Starfire' had now become the official title for all the top of the range 98s, which now had power steering and electric windows.

Above: 1957 Pontiac Star Chief. Identified by four stars on the rear fender, missile-shaped inserts, and full wheel disks, the Star Chief's power came from Pontiac's 270hp 347cu in V8.

Left: 1957 Imperial Crown. The Imperial Crown hardtop sedan featured the high flying tailfins that were all the rage at the time. Inside was a lavishly equipped interior while under the hood was Chrysler's meaty 392cu in 325hp Hemi V8.

Above: 1957 Pontiac Bonneville. The Bonneville name was first used in 1957 for a special fuel-injected convertible Pontiac model with massive fins at the rear, chrome wheel trims, chrome side mouldings and a wraparound windscreen. The following year a coupe was added to the range. Power for both cars came from either a 255hp or 285hp V8.

Right: 1957 Chrysler 300C. Now in its third year, the C edition of Chrysler's 300 series held on as the fastest and most powerful production car in the US. This 1957 version had a completely new grille. On the whole, exterior moldings were kept to a reasonably discreet minimum.

Left: 1957 Plymouth Belvedere. With newly introduced torsion-bar front suspension, the 1957 Plymouth Belvedere had fine road manners to march the performance potential of its 301cu in 215hp Hemi V8. Plymouth's most popular model, over 280,000 Belvedere models were produced that year.

Below: 1957 Dodge Coronet. Dodge produced some very sleek looking machines in 1957. They were longer, lower and wider than any previous Dodge, and were finished off at the rear with an impressive pair of fins. Front torsion bar suspension was introduced to improve both ride and handling.

Right: 1957 Plymouth Fury. Restyled for 1957 with extravagent fins, acres of chrome, and four headlights, the Fury — only produced as a two-door hardtop — was also modified mechanically with a new front suspension system and either 235hp or 290hp V8 power units.

Below: 1958 Chevrolet Biscayne four-door sedan. The Biscayne was offered in two- and four-door sedan body styles though the Brookwood station wagons actually had exactly the same trim and specifications. Prices started at $2,236.

Above: 1958 Ford Thunderbirdbird. The four-passenger 'Square Bird' Thunderbird was introduced in 1958, offered as either hardtop or convertible. These new T-birds were 18in longer and 1,000lb heavier than their predecessors, with a distinctive honeycombe grille in the bumper and round the tail-lights.

Left: 1958 Edsel Citation. The Ford Edsel was first introduced in the USA in September 1957, but despite its attractive lines and distinctive horse-collar grille, it failed to achieve the positive response that Ford executives had expected. The marque was officially discontinued in November 1959.

Right: 1958 Chevrolet DelRay. The DelRay was Chevrolet's entry-level auto in 1958, completely restyled and re-engineered to provide a longer and lower body than before. Though the interior trim was basic, and the cheaper 145hp straight six engine option underpowered, the DelRay could be specified with a 185hp 283cu in V8 whose power output was better suited to the car's size and weight.

Below Right: 1958 Packard Hawk. First introduced in 1958, the Packard Hawk was undeniably quick, thanks to its 275hp 289cu in V8 and light weight. Perhaps most remarkable about its memorable styling are the bizarre bolt-on fibreglass nose section, the exaggerated tail fins and the arm rests fitted to the top of the doors. This was to be Packard's last car.

Far Right, Top: 1958 Dodge Coronet. The Coronet was fitted with Chrysler's Red Ram 326cu in V8 for 1959 and was also offered with a wide range of oddball options including Co-Pilot Speed Warning and the self-dimming Mirror-Matic.

Far Right, Bottom: 1958 Imperial Crown. For 1959 the Imperial Crown's front grille was revised but far more significant was the adoption of Chrysler's new 413cu in 350hp V8 engine. Perhaps because of its elevated sticker price of $5,403, only around 1,700 examples were sold.

Right: 1958 Edsel Pacer. The Pacer was the third division Edsel model range — which saw Citation at the top, followed by Corsair, Pacer and Ranger entry level versions. Pacer and Ranger shared bodies that were smaller than that of the Citation and Corsair.

Below Right: 1958 DeSoto Adventurer. One of the innovations of the DeSoto Adventurer was the standard fitment of front seats that swiveled through 40 degrees to make getting in and out easier.

Far Right, Top: 1958 Plymouth Custom Suburban. With sales of 120,000 units in 1959, the Plymouth Custom Suburban continued to draw a strong following. The vast rear fins are less noticeable on wagon derivatives than on sedans and coupes but all models shared a restyled front, with a brighter grille and strangely shaped eyelids over the headlamps.

Far Right, Bottom: 1958 Buick Roadmaster Convertible. The Roadmaster remained Buick's prestige model during the 1950s. The car was made yet more distinctive around 1955 with the adoption of bright chrome fender bands and a golden 'Roadmaster' name plate on the hood. The Roadmaster's 236bhp V8 was mated to Buick's Dynaflow transmission.

Above: 1958 Pontiac Bonneville. The Bonneville Custom line was Pontiac's premier offering in 1958. Both Convertible and Sport Coupe models were offered, all fitted with four-barrel 370cu in V8s pushing out 240hp.

Right: 1958 Ford Fairlane 500 Sedan. Prior to the launch of the Galaxie, the Fairlane 500 represented Ford's top trim level. Though its body was carried over from the previous year, new twin headlights gave the 500 a more futuristic appearance.

Above: 1959 Chevrolet Biscayne. Chevy's entry-level auto in 1959, the Biscayne was restyled to offer wider and longer bodies, a new radiator grille, what was described as seagull-wing rear styling and larger glass area.

Left: 1959 Cadillac 62 Series Convertible. By 1959, Cadillac was not just a car but a cultural symbol. This year saw the culmination of the flamboyant style of 1950s car design. The tailfins were larger than ever, with its twin bullet taillamps, distinctive rooflines and new grill patterns providing the now infamous 'Batmobile' look.

Right: 1959 Buick Electra 225. The Electra 225 got its name from its stretched 225in body which housed more creature comforts than ever before. The Convertible had a leather interior and power hood, while Sedan and Hardtop versions gained power windows and a deluxe interior treatment.

Below: 1959 Rambler Ambassador. AMC's 1959 Ambassador was little changed from the previous year when it was first introduced. The new full-sized model enjoyed good sales successes, with over 400,000 sales in 1959 alone, helping AMC to fourth position in the auto sales league.

Above: 1959 Ford Fairlane 500 Skyliner. In 1959 Ford won a Gold Medal at the Brussels World Fair for the exceptional beauty of its cars. The Fairlane 500 Skyliner was also noted for its practicality, not least the way in which electric motors were employed to lower and raise the roof.

Left: 1959 Rambler American. This was AMC's compact model whose plain but functional styling dated back to 1954. Sticker prices started at just $2,098.

Right: 1959 Edsel Corsair. The long, low and undeniably stylish Ford Edsel Corsair had a 332cu in V8 under its hood producing 225hp, so it also had performance to match its looks. Yet the Edsel failed to find sufficient following in the marketplace and was discontinued in 1959 after just 110,847 had been built.

Below Right: 1959 Chevrolet Impala. Big and brash, the 1959 Impala was offered with both six- and eight-cylinder engines and in a range that included four-door sedan, four-door hardtop coupe, two-door hardtop coupe, two-door convertible, and Nomad station wagon.

Far Right, Top: 1959 Ford Galaxie Skyliner. The supremely elegant Ford Galaxie was produced by taking the roof line of the Thunderbird and attaching this to the Fairlane 500's body. The Skyliner retractable hardtop model was only available fitted with Ford's 200hp 292cu in V8.

Far Right, Bottom: 1959 Dodge Custom Royal. By 1959, Dodge was even lower, longer and wider than before. Its fins were still there, larger than life, and the brows over the headlights had grown too. The Custom Royal was still at the top of the series, and Dodge had introduced a rare air xsuspension system, an option that wasn't a great success.

Right: 1959 Cadillac Sedan
DeVille. While its higher roof
line detracted from the
undeniable elegance of
other 1959 Cadillacs, the
Sedan DeVille had masses of
interior space. Power came
from a 390cu in 325hp V8
and prices started at $5,498.

Below: 1959 Cadillac
Eldorado. The Eldorado
range for 1959 was confused
by Seville, Biarritz, and 6900
models which varied in levels
of trim but all shared
Cadillac's 345hp V8.
Perhaps the most outstanding
of all was the Eldorado
convertible, particularly when
specified with contrasting
interior trim.

Above: 1959 Ford Fairlane 500 Galaxie Sunliner. The Sunliner — available with both six- and eight-cylinder engines — was enormously successful, accounting for around 10% of all Galaxie sales — nearly 49,000 in 1959 alone.

Left: 1959 Cadillac Series 62 Coupe. The 1959 Cadillac summed up all that was best — and most extreme — about American auto styling at its zenith. Massive tailfins, twin headlights and elegant pillarless roof designs all combined to produce a classic.

The 1960s

The fins and chrome of the 1950s did not die out overnight once the new 1960s decade started. The adornments simply got a little less extravagant, perhaps in response to events in the world outside that greatly affected the American people: the Cold War against Russia and the shooting down of Gary Powers in his U-2 spy plane, the failed Bay of Pigs invasion of Cuba, the assassination of President John F. Kennedy, and race riots in many cities.

Another influence, rather closer to the heart of the Detroit motor industry, was the increasing success of smaller cars, the majority of which were imported from Europe. Imports already held 10% of the market at the start of the decade, and when local manufacturers American Motors and Studebaker moved into the compact market with the Rambler and the Lark respectively — both of which were extremely successful — the Big Three had to respond.

GM launched the Corvair, Ford the Falcon, and Chrysler the Valiant in the

early part of the decade and enjoyed immediate success — enough to actually reduce imports year on year and ensure that domestic manufacturers once more enjoyed over 90% of their home market. It would not be until the end of the 1960s, when the Japanese started selling in earnest, that imports once again topped the 10% mark.

Interestingly, as the decade progressed, even though the American car buying public had shown a distinct demand for smaller, compact, and inexpensive cars, all the Detroit manufacturers started increasing the size of the cars again. Even though the Ford Falcon, for example, was selling over 500,000 units a year at its peak, Ford and its main rivals all introduced larger 'small' cars towards the end of the 1960s. Ford's Fairlane and Mercury's Meteor, Buick's Special, and Chevrolet's Chevy II are all examples.

Corvair moved in a different direction in order to boost public interest and increase sales. It introduced a Corvair Club Coupe, a sporty two-seater with bucket seats based on the original Corvair, which quickly became responsible for a full two-thirds of all Corvair sales.

The other makers were not slow to recognize that the American public wanted more choice and was prepared to pay for speciality models. GM launched the Plymouth Barracuda, Studebaker the Avanti, and Buick the Riviera in order to benefit from the new demand for sporty looking cars.

But it was Ford that really won the day. Its response was the Mustang, an all new sports car with a long aggressive looking hood, short rear, and bucket seats. Americans simply could not get enough of it and a full 500,000 examples were sold in its first year.

With the Ford Thunderbird and the

Above: 1960 Chevrolet Impala. Chevrolet's 1960 Impala was a smart car, with triple taillights and a vertically ribbed aluminum rear beauty panel.

Above: Chevrolet Impala. The convertibles were the only models without simulated vents on the lower rear window moldings.

Chevrolet Corvette, both of which were first launched in the 1950s and both of which were still going strong, these new models dominated Detroit's advertising and publicity during the decade and encouraged yet more speciality cars to be introduced — such as AMC's Marlin and then Javelin, Oldsmobile's Tornado, the chevy Camaro, and the Pontiac Firebird and Grand Prix.

Just as important in the development of the American car industry as all these sleek looking cars, however, was a very ordinary looking one — the Pontiac GTO. It was during the development of the Pontiac Tempest — an ordinary sort

of sedan — that one of the engineers noticed that Pontiac's 389cu in V8 was the same size and shape as the 322cu in unit planned for the car. Chief engineer John DeLorean, who was to come to fame later on in the development of his own ill-fated DeLorean sports car, immediately authorised the development of a prototype fitted with the larger and more powerful engine. And to make the extra 75bhp go that much further, he also authorised the weight of the car to be reduced by removing as many of the extras as possible. Uprated suspension, better brakes and a four-barrel carburetor were specified in a Tempest options package that became known as GTO — Gran Turismo Omologate.

The GTO was an immediate success, not least because it offered genuine performance at an added cost of less than $300. The price include a blacked out grille, bonnet scoops, and wider tyres that demonstrated that the GTO was something out of the ordinary.

Pontiac expected to sell up to 5,000 units but actually sold over 30,000 in 1964, 60,000 in 1965 and 84,000 in 1966. The GTO represented the start of America's muscle car craze.

However, performance and style were not the only considerations on Detroit's horizon during the 1960s. In fact it was actually in 1960 that the State of California first mandated that all new cars sold there had to be fitted with special exhausts which would reduce the emission of polluting gasses.

Congress than got in on the act and in 1963 passed its Clean Air Act, and followed up in 1965 with the Motor Vehicle Air Pollution Control Act and in 1967 with the Air Quality Act. The result would be that motor manufacturers could no longer chase performance at any cost. They would from now on have to find a balance between the requirements of the new legislation and their understandable desire to offer optimum performance levels.

A second issue, that of safety, also made its mark during the 1960s. As more Americans bought cars, so more of them became involved in auto accidents and official fatality rates showed that while there had been some 37,000 deaths annually at the start of the 1950s, this had risen to close to 50,000 by the mid 1960s.

It was the State of Wisconsin that

Below: 1960 Ford Galaxie Starliner Sport Coupe. Long, low, and mean looking, the 1960 Ford Galaxie Starliner Sport Coupe was a virtually new model from the ground up, sharing only engines (six- and eight-cylinder) and transmissions from previous year Fords.

took the lead, insisting that all new cars from 1962 must be fitted with seat belts. Most other States passed a similar law the following year and then Congress took up the challenge, setting its own standards for cars it bought for federal government use. These included seat belts, rear view mirrors, dual braking systems, and even sun vizors.

Shortly after, the Highway Safety Act and the National Traffic and Motor Vehicle Safety Act became law in 1966 and one of its first effects was to set up a National Highway Safety Bureau which set to work developing mandatory vehicle safety standards.

But if all this new legislation was starting to cause headaches in Detroit, by the end of the decade, senior executives had yet more to contend with. While immediately post-war imports had topped the 10% mark, the success of America's own compact and speciality

cars during the early 1960s had seemed to have turned the tide.

Yet by the end of the decade, imports were once again creeping up, led by Volkswagen's Beetle which enjoyed ever increasing success and which actually accounted on its own for 50% of all imports to the United States. In 1969, the year in which Neil Armstrong walked on the moon and it seemed there was nothing the Americans could not do, imports topped the one million mark.

And, critically for the Big Three Detroit manufacturers, the maker in second place was Toyota, the Japanese giant that was just beginning to get its act together on a global scale. Toyota would lead a massive influx of Japanese imports during the following decade and change the face of the American auto industry irreversibly.

1960 Oldsmobile Super 88. The chic and slimline Oldsmobile middle series Super 88 Holiday two-door hardtop had been the company's second most popular car in 1959. Its super sleek styling meant it looked fabulous, but wouldn't break the bank. Sadly the most exciting piece of standard equipment was the deep twist carpeting. Oldsmobile's 'shark' fin look disappeared in 1960. The 'Batmobile' fins had been flattened to give the cars a more horizontally wingy, angular appearance. This was the last year that Oldsmobile kept its traditional three series format of full-size cars.

Above and Right: 1960 Imperial Crown Convertible. Its imposing presence meant that drivers of the 1960 Imperial Crown would never go unnoticed. From the front, a massive grille and swept-up fenders announced its approach, while from the rear the Imperial's enormous humpback fins housing gunsight tail-lights were an equally impressive sight.

Above and Left: 1961 Studebaker Lark Regal. At a time when Studebaker was struggling commercially, the Lark compact sedan offered some hope of sales success. It used Studebaker's reliable 112hp straight six engine in a body that was sensible and practical, though sadly lacking in elegance.

1961 Pontiac Tempest. The Tempest had all that was Pontiac in its design: twin grilles, sculptured body panel, and a V-contour hood. Its integral body and frame and integrated rear suspension were technically innovative, as was the torque tube drive.

Right and Below: 1959 Pontiac Bonneville. Bonneville was Pontiac's top line, and it made sure people knew this by putting golden nameplates on the left hand grille along with bright metal molding on the spears. Triple tail lamps were another distinguishing feature.

Above and Left: 1961 Buick Station Wagon. Gentle body styling contributed toward a slimmer and less bulky looking style for the 1961 Buick Special range. This went down well with the car-buying public and sales of Buick's smaller cars were strong that year. The station wagon could be ordered in both six- and eight-passenger versions.

1961 Lincoln Continental. Aircraft-carrier styling and barge-like dimensions were the primary characteristics of the imposing, sleek, and elegant 1961 Lincoln Continental. Specification levels were fast increasing, with standard power brakes, power steering, automatic transmission, radio, power door locks, and power windows; 65% of customers also requested air conditioning.

Right: 1960 Ford Thunderbird. 1960 saw the last of the 'Square Birds' with their highly sculptured body lines. The most significant change on the 1960 model was the addition of a manually operated sun-roof. The grill design changed again — this time reverting back to the 1957 style.

Above: 1962 Ford Thunderbird. After the remodeling the previous year, the 1962 Thunderbird was barely touched. The Thunderbird convertible had a fiberglass tonneau cover out on the back seats to make sure that a suitably sporty look was maintained. There was also an addition to the family — the Sport Roadster.

Below Right: 1963 Ford Thunderbird. Although the 1963 Thunderbird had the same body as the 1961-62 model, it is the most easily recognizable of the series. The difference was made by a mid-body feature line which dipped down near the back of the front door. A limited edition Landau was introduced with an all-white interior, normally called the Monaco.

Left: 1964 Ford Thunderbird. The Thunderbird was completely restyled once more in 1964. This time it got longer hoods, shorter roof lines and highly sculptured side panels. The front end became more aggressive looking, with a larger power dome on the hood. Sadly, the factory built Roadster was no more.

Below Left and Below: 1966 and 1967 Ford Mustangs.

Above and Right: 1961 Chrysler 300G. Chrysler's mighty 300G lost the option of a four-speed manual transmission in 1961 — all models were sold with automatic transmission only. Power came from the ram-inducted 413cu in V8 producing either 375 or 400hp according to specification.

Above: The Chevrolet Corvair Monza Club Coupe, introduced in 1961, was a revelation for Chevrolet. It outsold every other Corvair model, and was marketed as an economical sports car rather than a small compact. Bucket seats were its other strong selling point.

Left: 1962 Buick Wildcat. The Wildcat sport coupe was part of the Invicta range, but featuring a special steering wheel, centre console and vinyl bucket seats. Power came from an uprated 325hp versions of the Buick LeSabre's 401cu in V8.

Right: 1962 Buick Wildcat.
List price of the sportier
Wildcat was $3,927 against
the standard Invicta hardtop
coupe's $3,733 sticker price.

Below Right and Far Right,
Top: 1962 Rambler
American. Though by now
built at a brand new plant
in Ontario, Canada, the
1962 Rambler American was
hardly changed from the
1961 vintage, but that did
little to damp down enthusiasm for the marque. Rambler
sold some 435,000 units that
year, of which the compact
American contributed
136,000 sales.

Left: The 1962 Chevrolet
Corvair Monza Spyder
made its debut in 1962.
Technically it was an options
package, including a 150hp,
turbocharged version of
the Corvair engine. The
Spyder package was generally
treated as a separate model,
however.

The Pontiac Bonneville had all the standard equipment on the Star Chief, but combined with a little hint of comfort and luxury. Rear foam cushions, padded dashes and courtesy lamps were all available with the Bonneville, as well as Morrokide upholstery.

Far Left, Top and Bottom, and Left: 1962 Chevrolet Impala. The Impala line included Chevrolet's top models. Bright aluminum front seat end panels were one of the pieces of standard equipment that distinguished them from the lower priced ranges, as were extra plush interiors with embossed vinyl headings.

Below: 1962 Ford Falcon. Ford's compact 1962 Falcon line was essentially a carry-over from the previous year. Available as two- and four-door sedan and two- and four-door station wagon models, the Falcons were all powered by Ford's 144cu in 85hp straight six engine.

Right: 1962 Ford Falcon. The Falcon was never particualrly quick, but it was practical and relatively inexpensive, and therefore popular enough to rack up just under 400,000 sales that year.

Below: The 1962 Chrysler 300H, based on a 122in wheelbase and powered by Chrysler's vast 413cu in V8, proved highly successful thanks to the new styling that eradicated the fins of the past.

Left: So popular was the 300H that production volumes were up over 33% on the previous year, despite a sticker price that topped the $5,000 mark.

Below: 1963 Buick Riviera Available only as a stunning sports coupe model, the 1963 Buick Riviera was the most expensive car Buick then produced, with a sticker price of $4,333. Nevertheless, 40,000 customers took delivery that year of one of the 325hp, 401cu in V8 Rivieras.

Above: 1963 Buick Riviera.

Right and Far Right, Top: 1963 Studebaker Hawk Gran Turismo. The Studebaker GT Hawk, although based on the Starliner Coupe first launched in 1953, was restyled in 1962. For 1963 a more powerful range of engines was offered, starting with the standard 210hp 289cu in V8, but also encompassing both 240hp and 290hp superchanged derivatives.

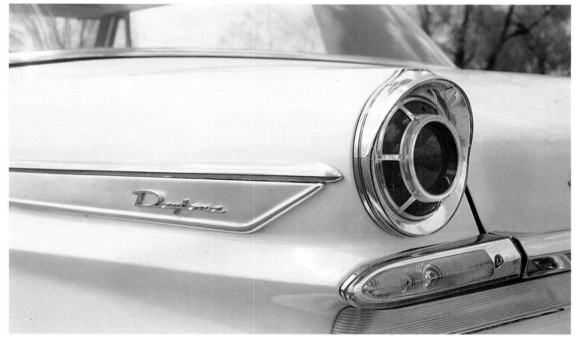

Above and Left: 1963 Studebaker Daytona Lark. The Lark had been a lifeline for Studebaker in the late 1950s, but the compact car's success could not be maintained once the big three auto makers brought out rival compact sedans. Into the 1960s sales steadily declined, despite the impressive performance of the 180hp 259cu in V8 Lark VIII.

1963 Studebaker Avanti. To prove its performance potential, Studebaker produced a 575bhp one-off version of the Avanti Coupe which achieved 196mph at Bonneville. The standard road-going version was fitted with either a 240hp 289cu in V8, or a supercharged 290hp version that was good for a top speed of 124mph.

Right, Below and Far right: 1964 Buick Riviera. Having launched the classic Riviera only a year earlier, Buick decided not to make major changes to the highly successful hardtop coupe. The brightwork changed a little, with fake rear fender cooling vents picked out with chrome, and the supremely elegant wheels now featured a stylized 'R' on the center of the wheel covers.

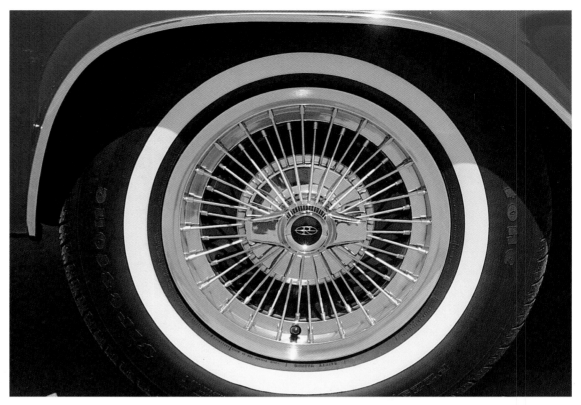

Below: 1964 Ford Falcon Sprint. Ford's motto for 1964 was 'Total Performance', and this was reflected on the Falcon Sprint in terms of its restyled and more aggressive grille and bodywork. Sprint models were produced only with V8 engines and with five-passenger accommodation, with front bucket seats. Both Spring hardtop and Sprint convertible models were available as the flagship models of the Falcon range.

Left: 1964 Ford Falcon Sprint.

Below Left and Below: 1964 Ford Galaxie. A new grille and sculpted lower body panels characterized the restyled 1964 Ford Galaxie. Though it was possible to buy a base Customer Galaxie fitted with a 138hp straight six engine, by far the most desirable model was the Galaxie XL, which featured bucket seats, a floor-mounted gear lever, and a generally sportier image to match its impressive 425hp 427cu in. V8.

The 1964 Lincoln Continental was even larger in 1964, reaching 216.3in in length and 78.6in in width. The front grille was amended and a new dash was specified, but otherwise styling changes were minor. Interior specification levels remained high although a new option of a moveable steering wheel provide unpopular.

Right: 1964 Excalibur Roadster. Taking a Studebaker Avanti V8 engine and a Lark Daytona chassis as a starting point, designer Brooks Stevens developed the Excalibur Roadster, a Mercedes-Benz SSK look-alike, in 1964. Originally planned as a Studebaker special, in the event Studebaker decided its retro styling did not fit in with the company's image and so Stevens formed SS Automobiles and put it into production himself — but by now fitted with a 327cu in Chevrolet V8.

Below and Far Right, Top: 1964 Oldsmobile Convertible. Oldsmobile decided that 1964 was its Year of Change. The F-85 Cutlass was redesigned and grew 11in in length. Having once been a compact, the F-85 was now a confirmed intermediate size. New engines were also specified, a 225cu in V6 producing 155hp, and a 330cu in V8 producing 250hp.

Left: 1964 Ford Mustang. The Mustang and filled the gap in the market for a small, cheap sports car. Born from the embers of the Ford Falcon, sharing its chassis and many of its components, although the Mustang's basic engine wasn't up to much, it could be fitted with virtually any Ford engine which gave it a significant advantage over its market rivals. Unsurprisingly, the Mustang was an instant hit.

Above and Right: 1965 Corvair Monza Convertible. By 1965, Monzas had replaced the Corvair 700 line as the mid-price Corvair models. The convertible came with a manual top and top boot as standard. The colors available were still limited to blues and grays, with optional aqua or black accents.

Left and Below: 1965 Chevrolet Impala Convertible. The 1965 Chevrolet Impala set itself apart from the crowd with rear fender extensions and additional wide, low, bright bodyside moldings with bright garnish moldings. It was a popular car and easy to spot in a parking lot.

Right and Below: 1965
Pontiac GTO Coupe. The
GTO was essentially a
Pontiac Tempest LeMans. It
was fitted with a standard V8,
but was identified by GTO
lettering on the left-hand
grille, rear fender sides, and
on the deck lid too. The
GTO also had elongated
V-shaped badges behind the
front wheel openings.

Far Right, Top: 1965
Excalibur. Not only was the
Excalibur designed to look
like the pre-war Mercedes-
Benz SSK, but it also
employed at least one of the
original component suppliers.
Unable to source the flexible
exhaust pipes in the USA,
designer Brooks Stevens
tracked down the original
SSK supplier in Germany and
placed an order there.

Below: 1965 Ford Mustang. Given its initial success the previous year, Ford made few changes to the Mustang in 1965. A fastback body, called the 2+2, was added to the hardtop and convertible choice and it was fitted with a set of louvers for ventilation, instead of rear windows. Mustang celebrated its first birthday with record sales levels.

1965 Plymouth Barracuda. Based on the Valiant, the Plymouth Barracuda looked good but for the most part failed to deliver on the performance front. Base models were fitted with an asthmatic 101hp six-cylinder engine that was later superseded by a slightly more powerful 145hp derivative. In truth, only the 273 cuin V8 producing 235hp was truly worthy of the Barracuda name, though all Barracuda model benefited from interesting styling details.

Above, Right and Far Right, Top: 1965 Chevrolet Corvair. Chevrolet gave the Corvair a completely new body in 1965, taken straight from the pages of the Italian school of industrial design manual. It was in its detail design that the Corvair stood apart from the crowd.

Left: The 1965 Thunderbird was, for the most part, identical to the 1964 model. A few extras were introduced, such as reversible keys and the keyless locking system. Vacuum-operated power door locks were also available.

Right and Below Right: 1966 Dodge Monaco. Dodge had brought out the Monaco in 1965. It was a speciality sedan launched to compete with the successful Pontiac Grand Prix. Dodge had chosen to make elegant simplicity as the Monaco's trademark, and in doing so it succeeded in producing a truly classy car.

Bottom Right: 1966 A.C Cobra. The AC Shelby Cobra started life as an out-and-out race car, but successful Texan race driver Carroll Shelby persuaded Ford to supply smallblock V8s to shoehorn into the lightweight aluminum chassis produced by the English AC company. The result was an instant classic — particularly the fearsomely powerful 427cu in 485hp version.

Left and Below: 1966 AMC Ambassador. For 1966 the AMC Rambler Ambassador gained a new roofline, larger tail-lights and new side chrome pieces. Though the Ambassador was doing fairly well in the showrooms, with total 1966 sales of over 34,000 units, only 1,798 examples of the $2,968 sticker price convertibles were sold.

Right: 1966 AMC Ambassador interior.

Below: 1966 Rambler Marlin. An Ambassador under the skin, the Rambler Marlin had a slick fastback body and offered a great deal of style even if this was not matched by outstanding performance from its relatively meager 145hp six-cylinder engine.

Above and Left: For 1966 features such as power steering and power brakes became optional rather than standard, but the price also dropped by around $550 to only $2,601.

Above: 1966 Pontiac GTO. The GTO line became an entirely separate series in 1966. It had its own distinctive trim on the new Tempest sheet metal. The GTO nameplate remained on the left hand side, and a single scoop appeared on the hood. The GTO had dual exhausts, heavy duty shock absorbers, springs and stabilizer bar.

Right and Far Right, Top: 1966 Pontiac Bonneville. Pontiac made its 1966 Bonnevilles easy to distinguish, with broad accent panels below the lower body crease and lettering on the left hand grille. Pontiac Bonnevilles were available as two- and four-door hardtops, two-door convertible, or four-door station wagon. Manual transmission cars were fitted with a 389cu in V8 producing 333hp, while Hydra-Matic auto versions produced 325hp.

Below Left: 1966 Chrysler 300 Convertible. Chrysler's 300s, now offered in four body styles, were fitted with a 325hp 383cu in V8. The new 300s may not have had the cachet of the earlier 300 'letter series' cars, but the public still was enthusiastic and Chrysler sold just under 50,000 units that year — nearly double the previous year.

Bottom Left: 1966 Ford Thunderbird. The Thunderbird got another makeover in 1966. It used the same body shell as before but the front grille was more aggressively angled and the rear tail-lights were extended to form a single continuous unit, with a back-up light used as part of the Thunderbird emblem.

Right and Below: 1967 AMC
Marlin. From the start of
1967 AMC invested large
sums in an attempt to rein-
vent itself. The Marlin was an
example: longer, lower and
wider than before but retaining its trademark fastback
roof. Sadly, the revisions did
little to reverse the Marlin's
sales slump.

Left: Chevrolet Camaro SS. Chevrolet launched the Camaro in 1967, propelling itself into the performance car race. The Z28 and SS performance packages were a particular hit with those with a need for speed. The Camaro would eventually replace the Corvair.

Below Left: Ford Mustang. 1967 saw the introduction of an all-new Mustang body. The styling, however, stayed almost exactly the same — due to popular demand. The same three body types remained, with the same three engine availabilities on offer, and an additional 320hp version.

Bottom Left: 1967 Ford Thunderbird. 1967 was another Thunderbird restyle year, with the front headlights hidden in a new full-width grill. A sedan option was also introduced — a first for the Thunderbird series. The four-door Landau had front opening rear doors, helpfully nicknamed 'suicide doors.'

1967 Cadillac Eldorado. A brand-new sporty front-wheel drive Cadillac Fleetwood Eldorado made its debut in 1967. The Eldorado appealed to those who wanted a combination of driving pleasure while ensconced in the lap of luxury. Its drivetrain layout meant the Eldorado could carry six passengers, despite being lower and shorter than any other of the Cadillacs.

Above, Above Right, and Right: 1968 AMC AMX
Still trying to revitalize its ageing range, AMC introduced the two-seater AMX sports car in 1967. It was fitted with a 290cu in 225hp V8 as standard, but a 390cu in 315hp V8 could be specified as an option. World Land Speed Record Holder Craig Breedlove set 106 world speed records with an AMC AMX and in celebration a limited number of AMX's were sold sporting a distinctive red, white, and blue paint job.

146

Below: 1968 Dodge Charger 440 Magnum. With a 440cu in 375hp V8 under its hood, the Dodge Charger 440 Magnum had stunning performance potential — potential that was hinted at by the vertical stripes at the rear of the car. Its semi-fast-back hardtop with flying buttress roof styling was immensely popular, and sales were sufficient to move Dodge up to sixth place in the USA sales league.

Above: 1968 Dodge Charger 440 Magnum.

Right: 1968 Dodge Charger. Redesigned for 1968, both Dodge Charger and Coronet models gained new 'coke-bottle' rear wings. Standard power came from a 318cu in V8 producing 230hp, though 290, 330, 375 and even 425hp V8s could be specified.

Above: 1968 Pontiac Firebird. Though fitted as standard with a 175hp 250cu in straight six, the Pontiac Firebird could be specified with a far more powerful V8. The Firebird 400 with that optional 335hp V8 under its hood was capable of acclerating from 0-60mph in just 7.6 seconds.

Left: 1968 Chevrolet Camaro Z28. Chevrolet wisely decided not to alter the Camaro too noticeably in 1968, after its launch the previous year. However, close inspection would reveal that new front and rear side-marker lights had been added, along with ventless door glass.

Above, Above Right, and Right: 1968 Oldsmobile 4-4-2 Hurst. 1968 was the year in which *CARS* magazine named the Oldsmobile 4-4-2 as its Performance Car of the Year. Its interior, decked out with fake wood, may have been a style-free zone, but the important specification was under the hood, where Oldsmobile's 455cu in 390hp V8 lurked. This was also the year in which the Hurst option was introduced. It consisted of unique black and silver paintwork, uprated suspension, and that 455cu in V8. In all, just 515 were manufactured, off-line by the Hurst Performance Products Co.

Below: 1969 Oldsmobile 4-4-2 Hurst. 1969 was the Oldsmobile 4-4-2's second year as a series, and three models were in production. Extra performance could be had from the W-30 package, based on the 'Force-Air' ram-induction engine. The special 4-4-2 was one of the fastest stock showroom domestic cars available to the public in 1969.

Right: 1969 Checker Marathon. One of America's best-known cars is the Checker — thanks to its near monopoly of the New York cab market for many years. It also sold cars for the general public, with its Marathon model first going on sale in 1961, based on the earlier Superba model. Fitted with a 327cu in 250hp V8 initially, Checker switched to 327cu in Chevrolet V8s in 1965. Never the most elegant car on the road, the Checker made up for its lack of street cred with genuine eight-seater capacity.

Below and Above Right: 1969 Chevrolet Chevelle. The Chevelle was Chevrolet's intermediate size car, and in 1969 it received new frontal styling. Low level Chevelles were identifiable by their thin rocker panel moldings and bright metal windshield.

Below: 1969 Pontiac Firebird Convertible. Since the Pontiac Firebird was restyled late in 1968, there were few changes in 1969. However, 1969 marked the launch of an important new derivative of the Firebird line — the Trans Am in March. Both Firebird and Trans Am were offered in two-door hardtop and two-door convertible versions.

Above, Above Right, and Right: 1969 Chevrolet Camaro Rally Sport. Chevrolet made its Camaros longer and lower in 1969. Sport coupe and convertible styles were offered alongside a Rally Sport version which had a special black grille with concealed headlights and a triple-slot insignia on its retractable headlamp doors.

Left: 1969 Pontiac Firebird.

The 1969 Pontiac GTO was based on the LeMans model but with a 400cu in 350hp V8 under the hood. During the year a special even higher performance version was launched, known as 'The Judge.' With a ram-air engine producing 370hp, the hard-top Judge was capable of accelerating from 0-60mph in a scorching 6.2 seconds.

1969 Dodge Daytona Charger. Only 550 Dodge Daytona Chargers were built, intended for NASCAR racers. The massively protruding front concealed the headlights and the massive rear wing was designed to provide stability at high speeds — which was just as well as they boasted a top speed in excess of 200mph. Under the hood was a massive 440cu in 375hp V8.

Above: 1969 Cadillac Fleetwood Eldorado. By 1969 the Eldorado had a huge following, although Cadillac continued its other lines, making minor alterations to them every year, as usual. The Fleetwood Sixty was given a longer wheel base, as well as carpeted folding foot rests.

Right: 1969 Dodge Dart. Available as a hardtop or convertible, the Dodge Dart was fitted with a 275hp 340cu in V8. Available as a four-door sedan or two-door coupe, this was very much the economy performance car of its day, most particularly the special Dart Swinger 340 which lacked most creature comforts but concealed a 340cu in V8 under its hood.

Left: 1969 Dodge Dart interior.

Below: 1969 Ford Mustang. 1969 was a bad year for the Ford Mustang. Although a new body retained the basic Mustang image, all the minor alterations to its appearance seemed to erase its essential essence. Two new models were also added; the Grande, a more luxurious version of the hardtop, and the Mach 1, a variation on the fastback.

Above: 1969 Plymouth 440 Barracuda. Of all the Plymouth Barracudas, the fastback body style was by far the most polular. But what made this 1969 440 Barracuda particularly special was its mighty 440cu in big block V8 fitted with a 'six-pack' of triple two-barrel carburetors.

Right: 1969 Pontiac Trans Am. Standard engine of the 1969 Trans Am was the Ram Air HO 335hp V8, and the base transmission was a four-speed manual with Hurst floor shift. To make them stand out from the crowd, Trans Ams were painted white or blue with contrasting racing stripes. Both coupe and convertible models were offered at $3,556 and $3,770 respectively.

The 1970s

Below: 1970 Chevrolet Monte Carlo. Launched in 1970, the Monte Carlo was based on the Pontiac Grand Prix platform. Only a two-door hardtop coupe was available and it was positioned as a semi-luxury auto, with plenty of specification as standard.

The 1970s was the decade in which the American car makers faced enormous challenges, with fierce competition from Japanese imports on the one hand, and ever greater government control and legislation on the other. New regulations were brought in that severely tightened up in areas such as safety, exhaust emissions and — unheard of in the USA previously — even fuel economy.

It was a truly radical state of affairs that put Detroit under the spotlight as it tried to prove it was capable of reinventing the auto — which is exactly what President Jimmy Carter's administration called upon the big auto makers to do.

The industry also had to contend with a new tide of consumerism that swept over America during the decade. One of the leading lights was Ralph Nader, who in the mid-1960s had published a book called Unsafe At Any Speed, which relentlessly criticized the Chevrolet Corvair. During the 1970s he

turned his attention to the Ford Pinto and Mercury Bobcat, Ford's $2,000 subcompacts that were launched in 1970 to compete with ever increasing numbers of small Japanese imports. At first, they seemed a great success with over a quarter of a million sales in the first year. But the Pinto/Bobcat suffered a major design flaw in that its fuel tank was positioned between the rear axle and the rear bumper and this made it vulnerable in rear impacts. To make matters worse, the fuel filler had a habit of becoming dislodged in major impacts, causing fuel spillages and fires.

Ford was forced to redesign the car with greater rear end protection towards the end of the decade, a move that added considerable weight to the car and therefore reduced its fuel economy — ironically the Pinto's whole raison d'être. The company was also forced to recall over 1.5 million Pintos and Bobcats to amend the filler necks to prevent them being ripped out.

Though it was Ford who suffered in the case of the Pinto, all the manufac-turers took careful note of how in future they would have to pay far more attention to the demands — and the whims — of the consumer.

To make matters worse for the domestic auto makers, the world faced two energy crises during the decade and as a direct result the Japanese, who were already producing smaller and more fuel efficient cars, started rapidly increasing their share of the US market.

By 1975 Toyota had overtaken Volkswagen as the leading importer, even though it was VW who opened the very first transplant manufacturing site when it started building Rabbits in an old Chrysler factory in New Stanton. The Japanese — Toyota, Nissan, and Honda — were soon to follow suit and a generation of US baby boomers was more than happy to spend its dollars on these odd looking imports which used hardly any fuel in comparison with most US cars and which — crucially — displayed a level of build quality and reliability that none of America's major manufacturers could hope to match.

Above: 1970 Chevrolet Monte Carlo Sport Coupe. Though the standard engine for the Monte Carlo was a 250hp 350cu in V8, there was also an optional 330hp version available that transformed the Monte Carlo Sport Coupe derivative into a true wolf in sheep's clothing: 0-60mph acceleration was in the sub-eight second range.

Right: The Chevelle was Chevrolet's intermediate size range in 1970, available in sedan, coupe, station wagon and convertible guises. Top of the tree in terms of performance were the SS396 and SS454 (illustrated) derivatives which offered scorching performance.

What it all added up to was a puncturing of the balloon of Detroit's self-confidence. It manifested itself in a number of ways — perhaps most noticeably in the styling of 1970s' American autos . . . or lack or it. It was the dullest decade visually since before the war.

It also manifested itself in terms of size. When the Middle East oil producing countries effectively shut off supplies, first in 1973-74 and then again in 1979, America's response was to down-size — and fast. This was partly as a result of consumer demand for smaller and more economical autos; but also as a direct result of government legislation, initiated in 1970 when Congress enacted its Air Pollution Control Law.

This called for a 90% reduction in NOx emissions by 1976, which in itself was a hard standard for Detroit's engineers to meet. It was as a direct result of this legislation that the auto industry developed the catalytic converter, an expensive component, but one which successfully reduced exhaust emissions without starving the engine of all its power and performance.

But more legislation was to come in the form of the CAFE — Corporate Average Fuel Economy — standard, which demanded that average fleet economy should reach 18mpg by 1978 and 20mpg by 1980. For the major US auto makers, whose larger models still sported V8 engines under the hood, reaching this standard was always going to be like climbing a mountain.

To comply with CAFE — and to meet the growing demand from consumers for smaller and more economical cars — the major US auto makers all launched sub-compacts during the decade, examples being the Ford Pinto, the Chevrolet Vega, the AMC Gremlin, and the Chrysler Cricket.

American drivers may have been stunned at the first Arab oil embargo, which led to huge lines at the gas stations; and they may even have been starting to accept that maybe they would never again be able to enjoy cheap and plentiful energy as they had in the past. But they were not yet ready for a mass move into sub-compact cars, however admirable their fuel consumption figures might be. As a result, Detroit started yet another major engineering task — downsizing the rest of their models and introducing front wheel drive which allowed designers to offer greatly increased interior space in a smaller and lighter — and therefore more fuel efficient — bodyshell.

Sadly for American auto manufacturers, the decade was also to teach them a lesson in just how fickle consumer demand could be. When gas was in short supply and pump prices rose, buyers flocked to showrooms in search of smaller and more fuel efficient cars.

In fact, Detroit proved just how fast it could react when pressed. For example, following the first oil crisis of 1973-74 the price of a barrel of oil went up by some 400% and the price at the pump in the USA went up from an average of around 35 cents to nearer 60 cents. US consumers turned their backs on the large, heavy, gas guzzling monsters that they had been used to driving and demanded the sort of smaller, economical cars that the Japanese produced so successfully. In response to this changing pattern in consumer demand, GM was

able to launch its Chevette just a year later, in 1975, and then started downsizing all its other models, culminating in the introduction of its first front wheel drive cars — the Chevrolet Citation, Buick Skylark, Pontiac Phoenix, and Oldsmobile Omega X-cars.

In the meantime, however, the Arab oil-producing nations had once again started supplying as normal and, as soon as gas was readily available and pump prices fell to more normal levels, so the US consumer started demanding bigger, gas-guzzling cars again. For the auto makers, the 1970s were a decade in which they were continually trying to keep up with consumer demand trends, and rarely getting it right on the button.

For the first time, the 1970s proved to the US auto industry that demand for their products would not, and could not, keep increasing year on year. Competition from abroad became an inescapable fact of life and even competition at home resulted in the introduction of widespread rebate programs as the major manufactures desperately tried to maintain volume and market share.

Below: 1970 Oldsmobile Toronado Coupe. In 1970, as in the preceding years, the cream of the Oldsmobile crop was the front wheel drive Toronado. It was fully equipped with Turbo-Hydramatic transmission, power steering, power brakes, a V8 engine, and Deluxe steering.

Just how difficult the 1970s were became all too clear in 1979, when Chrysler was forced to go cap in hand to the US government to plead for a $1 billion loan just to keep the company afloat. In the event, Congress approved the loan because allowing one of America's largest auto makers to collapse was unthinkable. As later history has proved, this was a wise investment on the part of Congress because, under the direction of ex-Ford chief Lee Iacocca, Chrysler would thrive in the 1980s and 1990s.

But it was a close run thing, and a truly humbling experience not just for Chrysler, but for the whole of the domestic US auto industry.

Left: 1970 Chevrolet Corvette. A new grille design and square exhausts were among the relatively few exterior changes made to the 1970 Corvette. Standard engine was a 350cu in V8 producing 300hp but options included 370, 390, and 460hp versions, the latter powered by the LS7 three-carb 454cu in V8, which added $3,000 to the sticker price of $5,469 for the coupe and $5,129 for the convertible.

Below Left: 1970 Pontiac Firebird 400 Coupe. Power for the 1970 Pontiac Firebird 400 Coupe came from a 400cu in four-barrel V8 producing 265hp, mated to a three-speed Hurst floor shift transmission. It was distinguished on the exterior by long twin hood air scoops and Formula 400 nameplates.

Below: 1970 Oldsmobile Delta Hardtop. The next step in the full-sized Oldsmobile line arrived in 1970 with the Delta 88 Custom. It offered three models and the range was topped off by the two-door Holiday hardtop.

Bottom Right: 1970 Buick Estate Wagon. For the first time since 1964, Buick offered an estate wagon. Based on a LeSabre body, it shared engines with the Skylark and LeSabre (155hp 250cu in V6 or 260hp 350cu in V8). Many Buick estate wagons were specified with woodgrain effect on the body sides.

Left: 1970 Buick Gran Sport Coupe. This Gran Sport was supposed to be in the tradition of American muscle cars, but with its standard engine it wasn't up to much — unlike the Gran Sport 455 which sported a new big block V8 and Hurst transmission and turned out a hefty 350hp from its 455cu in.

1970 Plymouth Superbird Hemi. The Plymouth Superbird's massive rear wing and concealed front head-lamps continued to attract an enthusiastic following among those who truly understood the appeal of the muscle car. That year Richard Petty took 21 NASCAR victories in his Superbird, helping ensure that the Hemi-engined versions of the Superbird were by far the most desirable.

Above: 1970 Buick Skylark. Sharper styling and a larger, more open cabin area were the result of changes made to the Buick Skylark range for 1970. Sticker prices started at a reasonable $3,177 for the base two-door six-cylinder coupe, but even the most expensive Skylark Custom V8 Convertible was still only $3,656.

Right: 1970 Pontiac GTO Judge. A stunning piece of automotive art, the Pontiac GTO Judge may have been reaching the end of its days in 1970, but it still offered tremendous performance and a truly muscular image. Its 455cu in V8 pushed out 325hp.

Above: 1970 Oldsmobile Cutlass Supreme. Special Sebring yellow paint and a hotter 350cu in engine were used to liven up the Oldsmobile Cutlass range in 1970. The Cutlass Supreme models were a two- and four-door hardtop and an elegant two-door convertible.

Left: 1970 Chevrolet Caprice. Part of Chevrolet's full-sized line-up, the Caprice was sold only as a two- or four-door sedan and a four-door station wagon. In all, some 92,000 examples of the V8 Caprice line were sold in 1970.

Above: 1970 Chevrolet Chevelle. The Chevelle was Chevrolet's intermediate size range in 1970, available in sedan, coupe, station wagon, and convertible guises.

Right: 1970 Plymouth Hemi 'Cuda. The ultimate Plymouth 'Cuda of 1970 was the Hemi-engined option. With three carbs, the 340cu in V8 produced awesome performance, matched by the 'Cuda's aggressive paintwork and hood tie-downs.

Above: 1970 Chrysler 300 Convertible. With its standard 440cu in V8 producing 350hp, the Chrysler 300 had plenty of performance on tap. Nevertheless, a 375hp derivative was also available as an option. 300s were sold in two-door hardtop coupe, four-door sedan, and two-door convertible versions.

Left: 1970 Pontiac Trans Am. With its distinctive white or blue paintwork with contrasting racing stripes, the Pontiac Trans Am also stood out thanks to front and rear spoilers, side air vents, front air dams, a shaker hood, and rear end spoilers. 3,196 examples were built in 1970, and sold at a $4,305 sticker price, considerably less expensive than the contemporary Corvette.

Right: 1970 Buick Gran Sport Stage I Convertible. Buick's not entirely convincing 1970 Gran Sport was supposed to be in the tradition of American muscle cars. However, with its standard engine it wasn't up to much. An entirely different matter was the Gran Sport 455 which sported a new big-block V8 and Hurst transmission and turned out a hefty 350hp from its 455cu in. In addition, both Stage I and Stage II added performance options could be chosen, involving hotter cams, higher performance manifolds and carburetors, forged pistons, and revised gear ratios.

Below: 1970 Dodge Challenger. By 1970, Dodge had come up with an answer to the problem posed by the Mustang and the Camaro — the Challenger. It came either as a two-door hardtop or a two-door convertible. The R/T was the high perform-ance version. Sadly muscle cars were on their way out and the launch was rather too late.

Left: 1970 Buick LeSabre Custom. A modest facelift was given to Buick's lowest-cost full-size range in 1970. The LeSabre Custom, however, was a little more plush inside than the base LeSabre: four-door sedan, two- and four-door hardtop, and two-door convertible models were available.

Below: 1970 AMC AMX. 1970 was the final year for the original AMX, although the name would not be forgotten. It would be kept alive on the performance-image Javelin and Hornet-based models.

Above: 1970 AMC Javelin. The 1970s model of the AMC Javelin was basically the same as the AMX, but it had kept its own distinctive twin venturi type grille.

Right: 1970 Plymouth GTX with Hemi V-8. Only 7,748 Plymouth GTXs were produced in 1970, making it Plymouth's rarest car that year. Only hardtop versions were by now available, though it was possible to specify the impressive 'Air Grabber' hood with a 440cu in V8 underneath. Power output was 375hp or 390hp.

Left; 1970 Cadillac Coupe DeVille. After 1969's styles proved unpopular, Cadillac was back on form in 1970. It introduced a huge 8.2 V8 engine, dropping the Sixty Special, and the DeVille Sedan and convertible. The gas-devouring Fleetwood Eldorado even had an 8.2 badge to announce its engine size to all.

Below: 1970 Chrysler Newport Royal. The Chrysler Newport continued to earn solid support, selling over 100,000 units in 1970. All were fitted with V8 powerplants, with the standard engine producing 290hp from its 383cu in, and an optional 330hp being available for those prepared to spend a little more.

Left: 1970 Ford Maverick.
Ford's compact two-door
semi-fastback offered good
value for money with a
sticker price of under $2,000.
It was powered by a
170cu in straight six producing 105hp; a three-speed
auto transmission was
standard. In its first year
580,000 were sold in the US.

Below: The 1970 Lincoln
Continental was restyled for
1970 to make it look like the
Continentals of old. Power
came from a 460cu in 365hp
V8 with Select-Shift automatic transmission as standard.

Far Left, Top: 1970 Ford
Falcon. Such was the overwhelming sales success of the
Maverick in 1970 that sales
of the Falcon model fell off a
cliff. Its sole claim to fame
was that it was Ford's cheapest Fairlane model of 1970.

Far Left, Bottom: 1970
Mercury Cyclone GT.
Distinguished by its nose, the
air scoop on the hood was
just for show, performing
no useful function. Under
the hood was a 429cu in
360hp V8.

Right: 1970 Ford Mustang. The biggest change for Mustangs in 1970 was the return from double to single headlights. The rear was also given a light restyle, and the famous 351 'Cleveland' V8 engine was introduced. As for the interior, it got vinyl high-back bucket seats as standard.

Below Right: The 1970 Ford Thunderbird was given a new grille in 1970. It proved to be rather too delicate however — to the delight of those working in car insurance. The Thunderbird was longer and lower than before, and this was accentuated by a single horizontal line along its mid-section. It also had smart new color-coordinated wheel covers.

Bottom Right: The Ford Mustang was given a restyled body in 1971. It had a different-looking front end and a flatter roof shape which lowered the height of the car slightly. Emphasis was now being placed on performance, with the least powerful engine dropped from the option list.

184

Left; The 1971 Thunderbird was essentially the same as the 1970 model, with only the usual annual minor alterations to the grille, headlights and bumper.

Below Left: 1972 Ford Mustang.

Bottom Left: 1973 Ford Thunderbird. 1973 saw few modifications to the 1972 Thunderbird. It suspension system was refined, however, and the inside of the car was made more spacious. The bar type grille was replaced by an egg-crate one, giving the front a more dynamic appearance.

Above: 1971 Pontiac GTO. A new nose with large grille cavities and body-colored bumpers distinguished the 1971 Pontiac GTO from earlier models. The standard GTO hardtop coupe and convertible were fitted with a 300hp 400cu in four-barrel V8 but for a mere $395 more, customers could upgrade to 'The Judge' GTO option, which along with some extra external stripes, secured a 455cu in four-barrel V8 under the hood producing 335hp.

Right: 1971 Buick Centurion Sport Coupe. Replacing the Wildcat, the Buick Centurion range was first launched in 1971. An elegant two door coupe, a four-door hardtop and a two-door convertible were all offered, each fitted with Buick's 455cu in 315hp four-barrel V8.

Above: 1971 Buick Riviera Coupe. In a busy year, Buick also introduced the all-new Riviera coupe in 1971. Thanks to its standard 455cu in 315hp four-barrel V8, the Riviera's performance more than matched its macho style. Yet a higher performance option was offered — the Gran Sport Riviera, fitted with a 330hp 450cu in V8, uprated suspension and a revised Turbo-Hydra-Matic transmission.

Left: 1971 Cadillac Coupe DeVille. Cadillacs were restyled in 1971 with an emphasis on safety. This led to them growing bigger than ever before, and the sheet-metal bodies emphasized their size. Massive front bumpers were added to comply with new safety regulations. Compression ratios were altered too, to allow the cars to use low-lead or lead-free gasoline.

Above: 1971 Oldsmobile 4-4-2 Convertible. 1971 was the beginning of a decline in the high performance market, not only for Oldsmobile, but also for most other manufacturers, and it marked the end for the 4-4-2. 1971 was the last time it would have actual model status at Oldsmobile.

Right: Chevrolet Kingswood Estate Wagon. The full-size Chevrolets were not only restyled for 1971 — they also grew even bigger, most especially the station wagon whose wheelbase was extended still further. The Kingswood Estate was available with either 145hp 250cu in six-cylinder engine, or alternatively a substantially more powerful 255hp 400cu in V8.

Kingswood
Estate Wagon
By Chevrolet

VEGA
BY CHEVROLET

Above: Chevrolet Vega. The Vega was Chevrolet's all-new sub-compact for 1971. It was sold as a two-door sedan, two-door coupe or two-door station wagon. Power came from GM's 140cu in in-line four-cylinder engine turning out 90hp.

Left: 1971 Ford Torino Cobra. A proven success on the racetracks, the Ford Torino found some 260,000 buyers in 1971, despite the fact that there was little new on offer this year; the Torinos were effectively just 1970 bodies with some minor trim changes.

Above: 1971 Buick Riviera Coupe.

Right: 1971 AMC Hornet. In 1970, AMC replaced the Rambler with an old name and a new car. Hudson Motors had previously had a champion stock car called the Hornet, however, the new model was rather more conventional. The emphasis was on economy — it was really still the same old Rambler with a slightly more modern design.

190

Left: 1971 Chevrolet Chevelle SS. The Chevelle continued to be one of Chevrolet's biggest selling models during 1971 with over 330,000 examples sold during the year. Of these, just under 20,000 were the very special SS 454s, fitted with Chevrolet's massive 454cu in 365hp four-barrel V8.

Below: 1971 AMC AMX. AMC's new Javelin AMX for 1971 was a four-seater to replace the two-seater AMX that went before. The AMX was now the most luxurious of three Javelin trim levels — Javelin, SST and AMX. It was also the most powerful, thanks to a 245hp 360cu in V8 under its hood.

Right: 1971 Plymouth Road Runner. Plymouth's new 1971 'Fuselage' design was an immediate hit, but most impressive of all was the Road Runner, distinguished by a special performance hood, dual exhausts, uprated suspension, a 383cu in V8 pushing out 300hp — and a Beep-Beep horn in honor of the Road Runner cartoon character.

Below: 1971 Plymouth 340 Duster. Part of Plymouth's Valiant line-up, the 1971 340 Duster was the performance derivative complete with four-speed floor shift transmission, heavy duty suspension, Plymouth's 340cu in V8 producing 275hp and special go-faster stripes along the flanks.

Above: 1971 Dodge Charger: Completely restyled, the 1971 Dodge Charger now had a 115in wheelbase and was available in a wide range of hardtop and coupe semi-fastback derivatives. Standard engine was a 225cu in slant six or 318cu in V8, though Super Bees had a higher performance 383cu in V8 and the flagship R/T models had a 440cu in Magnum V8 under the hood that produced 370hp.

Left: 1971 Ford Brougham LTD. The sharp edges, concealed headlights, and clean design of the Ford LTD Brougham made a good initial impact. Under the hood was Ford's 351cu in 250hp V8.

Right: 1972 Cadillac Fleetwood 60 Special Brougham. 1972 was Cadillac's 70th anniversary, and one was even given to Russian premier Brezhnev by Richard Nixon. Cadillacs were still selling well despite now being more of an institution than an innovator. General Motors were still concerned with complying to safety standards in this year, leaving little room for major restyles.

Below: Chevrolet Corvette. Though its styling was little changed from the previous years, the 1972 Corvette did gain a Posi-Traction rear axle as standard. Total production of the $5,472 sport coupe was around 20,500 while production of the $5,246 convertible — now available with either white or black top — reached 6,500.

Above: 1971 Chevrolet Caprice. As Chevrolet's flagship model, the Caprice grew in size yet again in order to increase passenger space. All Caprice models — four-door sedan, two-door custom coupe, and four-door station wagon — were fitted with a 170hp 400cu in V8.

Left: 1971 Ford Pinto. A car that severely damaged Ford's image, the Pinto hatchback was intended to be a relatively inexpensive runabout and initial sales were good, despite the Pinto's unsophisticated four-cylinder engine and sparse interior. Later, it transpired that a badly designed fuel tank and fuel filler had a tendency to explode as a result of rear impacts and Ford was forced to recall all Pintos for costly modifications.

Above: 1972 AMC AMX. For 1972 the AMC Javelin AMX was distinguished from the Javelin SST by a different grille, sports steering wheel, rear spoiler, special wheels and a 304cu in V8 producing 150hp under the hood.

Right: 1972 Oldsmobile H/O Cutlass. A Hurst/Olds performance package was offered on Oldsmobile Cutlass coupes and convertibles in 1972 though the majority of Cutlass models retained a standard powertrain. Sadly for driving enthusiasts, out and out performance was losing out to the requirements of economy and lower fuel emissions during the 1970s.

Left: 1972 Pontiac Trans Am. The Trans Am, at $4,256, was over $1,000 more expensive than the Pontiac Firebird hardtop coupe on which it was based. Much of this was accounted for in trim and paintwork changes, but in addition the Trans Am had Pontiac's 455cu in 300hp V8 under its hood.

Below: 1972 Chevrolet Camaro SS. For 1972 the Chevrolet Camaro gained a new grille and revised bucket seats but a strike at the Lordstown Ohio assembly plant put the future of this model in considerable doubt. GM had to scrap many thousands of Camaro bodies because of the strike and came close to canning the whole Camaro and Firebird programme.

Right: 1972 Ford Mustang. By 1972, the Mustang was being referred to as Ford's 'Sports Compact'. Styling had remained more or less unaltered and it was now available in five two-door styles, two hardtops, two fastbacks, and a convertible. The additional engine options meant the Mustang was now more 'high performance machine' than cheap luxury auto.

Below: 1972 Ford Torino Gran Sport. With an even more pronounced 'Coke Bottle' style than before, the new Ford Torino range sold an astonishing 496,000 units in 1972,. The Gran Torino range consisted of the higher specification autos with the Gran Torino Sport also featuring a higher perfor-mance 140hp 302cu in V8.

Above: 1972 Mercury Comet Sedan. The major change to the 1972 Mercury Comet range was the adoption of body pin stripes. Despite there being a difference of only around $50 in the sticker price between the two-door sedan at $2,342 and the four-door at $2,398, 53,000 people opted for the cheaper model, while just 29,000 went for the four-door.

Left: 1972 Ford Maverick Grabber. The Ford Maverick series was unchanged in 1972 from the previous year but continued to sell well. In all over 250,000 were produced that year, of which the vast majority were the two-door sedan. Smallest selling, but most interesting in appearance was the two door Maverick Grabber which achieved just over 35,000 sales.

Right: 1973 Cadillac Eldorado Convertible. In 1973, the Indianapolis 500 was paced by a Cadillac Eldorado — something a Cadillac hadn't done since 1937. A blue sedan became the five millionth car Cadillac had produced, and as for the rest of them — they got new shock absorbing bumpers.

Below: 1973 Pontiac Grand Ville. The Pontiac Grand Ville was little different to other full size Pontiacs in 1973. It was available in four-door and two-door hardtop, two-door convertible, and four-door station wagon guises.

Left: 1973 Buick Century Luxus. Buick's new Century Luxus and Regal lines were the latest intermediate range of sedans, coupes, and station wagons introduced in 1973. The standard power unit was Buick's 350cu in 150hp V8 though a 190hp version of the same engine was available on the special Century Grand Sport Coupe. The bigger 455cu in V8 producing 225hp was available on Century Luxus and Regal models at extra cost.

Above: 1973 Pontiac Luxury LeMans. As its name implied, the Pontiac Luxury LeMans autos were the upmarket versions of the LeMans series. All had V8 power, and a higher level of specification than the entry level models.

Above: 1973 Pontiac Grand Am. A unique body-colored nose section, a high level of interior equipment, and a standard 400cu in V8 producing 170hp made the Pontiac Grand Am one of 1973's more distinctive offerings. 200hp, 250hp, and 310hp V8 engine options were available at extra cost.

Right: 1973 Mercury Cougar. The front end appearance of the Mercury Cougar was refined for 1973 but otherwise it was business as usual. Most popular model was the Cougar XR-7 which could be distinguished from the base model by different wheel covers and a vinyl roof.

Left: 1973 Ford LTD II. The major changes to the full size Ford ranges for 1973 — Custom, Galaxie, LTD, and LTD Brougham — were mandated by federal safety requirements, which led to the introduction of bulky and unattractive bumpers. The LTD was the top trim level that enjoyed such luxuries as deep cushioned seats, an electric clock and vinyl inserts on the side body panels.

Below Left: 1973 Pontiac Trans Am. What made the 1973 Pontiac Trans Am truly stand out from the crowd were its new hood graphics, designed to recreate an ancient Indian symbol but known more popularly as 'Chicken Graphics.' Under that hood was a 455cu in V8 producing 250hp in standard form, or an optional 210hp.

Bottom Left: 1973 Ford Mustang.

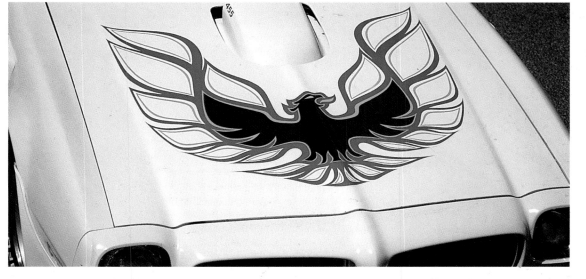

Right: 1973 Ford Pinto Squire Wagon. Although in essence the Pinto remained largely unchanged in 1973, like other auto makers Ford was forced to adopt 'parkbench' bumpers in response to new federal safety legislation. These bumpers added around one and a half inches to overall length.

Below: Chevrolet Camaro Sport Coupe. Restyled for 1974 with its grille angled forward, the Chevrolet Camaro continued to attract a high level of interest in the showrooms, with over 150,000 sold during the year. Six and eight-cylinder versions of the hardtop coupe were available, with the Z/28 version getting brighter graphics on both hood and rear trunk lid.

204

Above: Chevrolet Corvette Stingray Coupe. The rear bumper was removed to be replaced by a body-colored polyurethane unit and the rear of the Corvette became more angled during 1974. Standard power was still from a 350cu in 250hp V8 though the LS4 package could be ordered for just $250, which provided a 454cu in V8 producing 270hp.

Left: Chevrolet Caprice Classic Convertible. For 1974, Chevrolet's Caprice full-size models were changed in appearance to distinguish them from the Bel Airs and Impalas. The Caprice got a more sophisticated grille and new sheetmetal at the front that gave a sleeker more swept back look. All Caprices were sold with V8 engines only.

Above: Chevrolet Vega Kammback Estate Wagon. A new four-slot grille distinguished the 1974 Chevrolet Vega. Bumpers were also increased in size to meet federal regulations and this resulted in a three-nch increase in overall length. Standard power output remained at 72hp though a 75hp option was offered.

Right: 1974 Buick Riviera Sport Coupe.

Above: 1974 Cadillac Fleetwood Talisman. Perhaps the most ostentatious of all Cadillacs in 1974, the Talisman boasted four massive armchairs trimmed with Medici crushed velor, a massive center containing a writing set in the front and a vanity set in the rear and — for the truly wealthy — an optional all-leather package that cost a cool $2,450 over and above the already steep $11,337 sticker price.

Left: 1974 Cadillac Calais Coupe. Cadillacs had a substantial makeover in 1974. Modern technology and the gas crisis had overtaken them. The dashboard clock was now digital, and air bags were offered optionally, as well as a new range of luxury items. Sales dipped because of the political situation, but Cadillac's share grew.

Right: 1974 Buick Riviera Sport Coupe. Restyled for 1974, the Buick Riviera Sport Coupe gained a new more upright grille and a revised roofline. Though still fitted with Buick's 455cu in V8, its power output was on the way down, however: From 315hp at launch in 1971, to 260hp in 1973 and now down to 210hp. The following year, its output would be down still further, to 205hp.

Below: 1974 Ford Mustang. The crunch came in 1974, when the Mustang II replaced the original 1964 model. Although many ponycar fans were initially disappointed by the updating of their favorite design, the newer and smaller version sold much better than its larger predecessor.

Left: 1974 Ford LTD Pillared Hardtop. Refinement, luxury, and comfort were the watchwords of the LTD Pillared Hardtop. Quick, it was not — thanks to new safety legislation that added up to 350lb to the total weight of a typical auto, plus new emissions legislation that served to further emasculate the output of the Ford's 351cu in V8. Now producing a feeble 162hp, 1974 Fords were among the slowest autos produced by the company in many years.

Below: 1974 Plymouth Road Runner. As federal emissions laws effectively demanded reduced power outputs, the Road Runner's 440cu in V8 was producing only 275hp by 1974. As power dropped, so customers fell by the wayside and production fell to 11,555 units that year.

Right: 1975 Buick Skyhawk Hatchback Coupe. Buick's all-new sub-compact car, the Skyhawk was launched in 1975. Based on GM's H-Body platform used by the Chevy Monza, the Skyhawk had a Buick engine under the hood — a 231cu in V6 producing 110hp.

Below: 1975 Cadillac Seville. With Chrysler discontinuing the Imperial in 1975, Cadillac was left as King Car, as it was still managing to outsell the Lincoln. Changes were made to the headlights and the front, as the Cadillacs became squarer and more chiseled-looking. This was backed up by the massive 8.2 V8 engine which was still alive and well.

Above: 1975 Buick Apollo. Fully revised for 1975, the Buick Apollo and Skylark series were restyled to give them a European look. Though the standard engine was a 110hp 23cu in V6, a 260cu in V8 was also available — also producing 110hp. As a result, many buyers chose yet another option, a 350cu in V8 producing 145hp.

Left: 1975 Buick Riviera. Still Buick's top model, the $6,420 Riviera hardtop sport coupe continued to attract attention. Its front end, grille, and headlights were restyled for 1975 and overall the length of the Riviera was reduced by three or four inches.

Above: 1975 Pontiac Firebird Hardtop Coupe. Visually, 1975 Pontiac Firebirds were little changed from previously, though they did gain a new roofline and wrap-around rear window. The Chevrolet six-cylinder 250cu in 105hp unit was the base engine, but a 155hp 350cu in V8 was also available and later in the year a 200hp derivative was launched.

Right: 1975 Oldsmobile Starfire Hatchback Coupe. The subcompact, almost miniature Oldsmobile Starfire was introduced in 1975, even smaller than the Omega. The Starfire was based on the Chevy Monza, and its 97in wheelbase meant that it was now officially the smallest post-war Oldsmobile. The Starfires were made in Quebec, Canada.

Left: Chevrolet Monza 2+2 Coupe. One of Chevrolet's popular names from the past was reinvented in 1975 — the Monza appeared as a smartly styled sub-compact fastback 2+2 coupe that was built on a Vega platform. The Monza was a little longer and wider than the Vega and this provided room for a small-block V8 as an alternative to the breathless Vega 78hp fours.

Below: Chevrolet Cosworth Vega. Just 2,000 of the special edition Chevrolet Cosworth Vegas were built during 1975. Designed in England by famous race engineers Cosworth, its four-cylinder double overhead cam 122cu in 16V engine produced 120hp, a considerable improvement on the standard Vega's 78hp. Racing versions turned out 270hp.

Right: 1975 Bricklin SV-1. An investment by entrepreneur Malcolm Bricklin of $20 million resulted in what he described as the world's first safety sportscar. It featured gullwing doors and futuristic styling, and its large block Ford V8 promised good performance. In the end only 2,875 examples of the Bricklin SV-1 were ever built and the Canadian assembly plant was closed in December 1975.

Below Right: 1975 Chevrolet Caprice Convertible. 1975 was to be the last year that the Chevrolet Caprice convertible would be built. Some 8,350 of the elegant rag tops were sold during the year, all with 145hp 350cu in V8s under the hood, and all fitted with a high level of luxurious equipment. Sticker price that year was just $5,113.

Bottom Right: 1975 Ford Mustang. After the dramatic changes of 1974, the Mustang remained untouched in 1975, although an MPG series, carrying fewer standard options and a smaller price tag, was added to the range mid-season.

Left: The Ford Granada was launched in 1975 and sold over 300,000 units that same year. Based on the Maverick platform, it had European styling, a luxurious interior and good performance from its optional 351cu in two-barrel V8. Unfortunately for Ford, much of the Granada's sales success was at the direct expense of sales of the Mustang.

Below Left: 1975 Ford Gran Torino Brougham. Hardly changed from the previous year, Ford's Gran Torino range thundered on, clocking up impressive sales successes with a total of 159,000 sold. In fact the figure was higher by 102,000 units, but Ford chose this year to try to distance the Elite from the Gran Torino range and pretend it was a model in its own right.

Bottom Left: 1975 Ford Thunderbird. In 1975, the Thunderbird was given various new features as standard, such as the Sure-Trac rear-brake anti-skid device and the Hydro-Boost hydraulic brake boosting system. Air conditioning and AM/FM radio were now also standard.

Above: 1976 Chevrolet Monte Carlo. A three-bar grille and rather odd-looking twin headlamps set one on top of the other were the major styling changes on the Chevrolet Monte Carlo for 1976. The base power unit was a 305cu in V8 though both 350 and 400cu in V8s were also available.

Right: Chevrolet's Monte Carlo Landau was distinguished by its landau roof and body-colored mirrors. Other differences were minor, including different wheels, dual horns, and body stripes. The Landau cost $4,966 against the standard Monte Carlo's $4,673 sticker price.

Left: Chevrolet Chevette Hatchback Coupe. Perhaps the most important car launched by Chevrolet during 1976 was the Chevette Hatchback Coupe. Based on GM's European subsidiary Opel's Kadett model, this small two-door was at the forefront of a growing trend towards down-sizing in the wake of the oil crises. With a sticker price of only $2,899 at launch, the Chevette was aimed very firmly at Americans who had previously been tempted by imports from Japan and Germany.

Below: Chevrolet Monza Towne Coupe. The Monza got off to a great start following its introduction in 1975. Nearly 81,000 were sold during 1976 and it was voted Car of the Year by *Motor Trend* magazine. The base Towne Coupe was fitted only with Chevy's 140cu in four-cylinder engine, though other Monza derivatives could be ordered with either 262 or 305cu in V8s.

Right: Chevrolet Nova SS Coupe. Of the 330,000 Chevrolet Novas sold in 1976, just a handful — 7,416 — were the special SS Novas. Both coupe and hatchback SS derivatives were available, set apart from the crowd by a black grille and other black trim around the headlamps and windows. The biggest engine available was the 350cu in 165hp four-barrel V8.

Below and Far Right, Top: For 1976, the Buick Riviera Coupe gained not only a yet more comfortable interior, but more importantly, revisions to the engine, transmission, and final drive.

Left: 1976 Buick Electra 225 Limited. Both coupe and hardtop versions of Buick's upmarket Electra and Electra Limited were offered in 1976, sharing the Riviera's 205hp 455cu in V8. The Electra Limited four-door hardtop sedan had the privilege of overtaking the sticker price of the Riviera this year, and thus became Buick's most expensive auto.

Above: 1976 Buick Skylark Sedan. Though a 231cu in V6 producing 105hp was the standard power plant of the new compact Skylark range, customers could opt for a 110hp 260cu in V8 or either two- or four-barrel 350cu in V8s producing 140hp and 155hp respectively instead.

Right: 1976 Ford Mustang. The Mustang highlights in 1976 included fuel economy gains and a new sport exterior dress-up package for the Mach 1 and the 2+2. Two special option packages were offered — a new Stallion group for the younger customer and the infamous Cobra II.

Left: 1976 Pontiac Trans Am. For 1976, the Pontiac Trans Am was sold in just five body colors: Firethorn Red, Carousel Red, Goldenrod Yellow, Cameo White, and Sterling Silver. Power still came from the largest of Pontiac's V8 family, the 455cu in unit producing 200hp.

Below: 1976 Chevrolet Caprice Classic. Bel Air sedans and station wagons, the Impala sport coupe, and the Caprice convertible were dropped from Chevrolet's full-size line-up in 1976. But there were still some 13 models to choose from — seven Impalas and six of the rather more upmarket Caprice Classics.

Right: 1976 Excalibur Series. By 1976, the independent Excalibur sports car — unashamedly modeled on the pre-war Mercedes-Benz SSK — was no longer offered with a manual transmission option. Under the retro bodywork were Chevrolet Corvette mechanicals.

Below: 1976 Ford Pinto Stallion. Introduced in 1976, the Pinto Stallion was aimed squarely at younger drivers. It differed from standard Pintos in its silver paintwork, black moldings on the doors and windows, black hood, grille, rear panel and windscreen wiper arms. It also had upgraded suspension though engines were identical to regular Pintos.

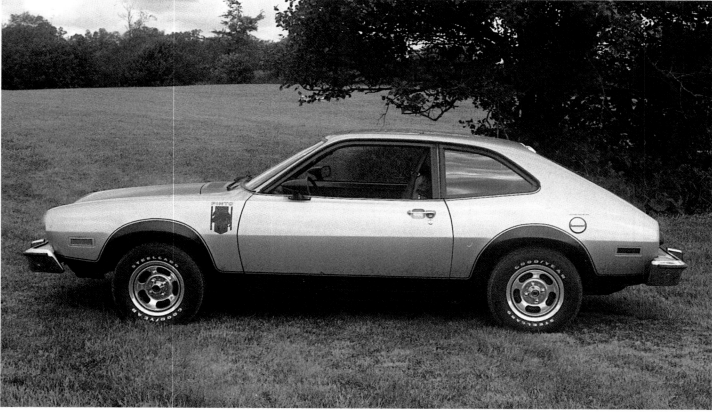

Left: 1976 Ford Elite Hardtop. Originally called the Gran Torino, the pillarless two-door hardtop sported an Elite badge in 1976. Its standard gold vinyl roof was matched by gold vinyl side body moldings though a half-vinyl roof could be specified. The Elite's standard base engine was a 351cu in V8 producing 152hp, though optional 180hp 400cu in or 202hp 460cu in V8s were also available.

Below: 1976 Lincoln Continental. Two distinct styles were available in 1976: the classic four-door sedan and the sportier looking coupe. Both Town Car and Town Coupe options were offered for those seeking yet more luxury but only one engine was fitted — Lincoln's 460cu in V8 producing 202hp.

Above: 1976 Mercury Comet Coupe. The new Comet Coupe replaced the former GT in the 1976 Mercury Comet line-up. With its distinctive two-tone paint job, special wheels and tyres, and bucket seats, it looked the part. It also performed well when the optional 302cu in V8 replaced the standard 200cu in straight six engine.

Right: 1976 Chevrolet Corvette. Sadly for its supporters, the Corvette convertible was dropped in 1976, leaving just the Stingray coupe to survive. Though the Corvette retained its fibreglass body, a new steel platform was adopted. This did nothing to hamper sales which reached a record level of 46,500 that year.

Right: 1977 Cadillac Coupe DeVille. 1977 was a landmark year for Cadillac. It celebrated its 75th anniversary and shaved almost half a ton off all full-size models — except the Eldorado. The Coupe DeVille was for "very special people," according to Cadillac, those who wanted plush pile carpet on the front and rear floormats, as well as on the lower doors.

Below: 1977 Cadillac Coupe DeVille. 1977 was a landmark year for Cadillac. It celebrated its 75th anniversary and shaved almost half a ton off all full-size models — except the Eldorado. The Coupe DeVille was for "very special people," according to Cadillac, those who wanted plush pile carpet on the front and rear floormats, as well as on the lower doors.

Below: 1977 Pontiac Ventura. With an upgraded interior and a new grille design, the Ventura range encompassed two-door coupe, two-door hatch coupe, and four-door sedan in both base and SJ series.

Left: 1977 Buick Le Sabre Custom Sedan. Even though the new 1977 Buick LeSabre was some 10in shorter and nearly 3in narrower than the model it replaced, it offered more interior space than before and more luggage space too. Versions of this same down-sized new B-Body were also used in the Pontiac Bonneville, Oldsmobile 88, and Chevrolet Caprice.

Bottom Left: 1977 Buick Electra. Though it still looked broadly similar to the Buick Electra of the previous year, in fact the new Electra was a full 10in shorter as Detroit's down-sizing phase moved into full swing. Plushest model of all was the Park Avenue derivative.

Below Left: 1977 Oldsmobile Cutlass Colonnade Coupe. After Oldsmobile's successes in 1976 when the Cutlass became the best-selling American automobile, the total number of Oldsmobile models was dropped by six in 1977, and a V6 engine launched to replace the old in-line six. The first wave of down-sizing also struck, with the full-size models now becoming "family size." The basic Cutlass Supreme Cruiser was discontinued.

Left: 1977 Ford Granada Ghia Coupe. Though similar externally to previous Granadas, the 1977 version was distinguished in being America's first domestic car to offer a four-speed with overdrive transmission. The more upmarket Ghia versions of the Granada had colored keyed vinyl bodyside moldings and special wire-wheel style wheel covers.

Below Left: 1977 Mercury Cougar Brougham. Having been totally restyled in 1976, few major changes were made to the appearance of the 1977 Mercury Cougar Brougham. The full line-up was two-door hardtop coupe, four-door hardtop, and four-door station wagon Cougars; two- and four-door hardtop Cougar Broughams; four-door station wagon Cougar Villager; and two-door hardtop coupe XR-7.

Far Left, Top: 1977 Ford Pinto. For 1977 the Ford Pinto was completely restyled to give it a sportier appearance. It was still offered as a two-door sedan, three-door "Runabout" hatchback and two-door station wagon. A 140cu in four-cylinder engine was standard but a sports pack could be ordered which included uprated springs, a tachometer, and a shorter gear lever to speed up changes.

Far Left, Bottom: 1977 Chevrolet Impala Custom Coupe. Nearly 11in shorter and 4in narrower than before, the 1977 Chevrolet Impala suffered the indignity of down-sizing alongside virtually every other full-size auto in America. However, clever design meant that the interior dimensions remained the same and the 600lb weight saving made significant improvements to fuel economy.

Left: 1977 Ford Mustang. No major style changes were imposed on the 1977 Mustang, although it was given some new color options and both the four-cylinder and V6 engines lost power. The notchback and the three-door fastback models were still the only bodystyles available.

Below Left: 1977 Ford Thunderbird. 1977 saw the end of the great and glorious Thunderbirds. The new models were smaller and largely based on the new LTD II. The chic sheetmetal look helped to disguise the shrinkage if not the reduction in standard equipment. More options than ever were now available, however, from radios to engines.

Bottom Left: 1978 Pontiac Trans Am. Little changed in either appearance or specification to previous years, the 1978 Pontiac Trans Am nevertheless remained by far the most popular of the Firebird series, clocking up 93,300 sales, more than the Firebird, Firebird Esprit, and Firebird Formula combined. A special Gold special edition Trans Am was introduced that year.

Far Left, Top: 1977 Ford LTD Country Squire. Biggest and most luxurious of all Ford's station wagons was the LTD Country Squire. It could transport six and their luggage in comfort, or alternatively a $134 option added a pair of dual-facing rear seats that boosted the Country Squire's carrying power still further.

Far Left, Bottom: 1977 Lincoln Continental. Though slightly restyled for 1978, the Lincoln Continental retained the earlier classic vertical chrome strip grille. During the year the standard 460cu in V8 was replaced by a more modern and efficient 400cu in V8 with the larger engine becoming an option. The sticker price remained below the $10,000 mark — at $9,636 for the sedan and $9,474 for the hardtop coupe.

Above and Right: 1978 Chevrolet Camaro Sport Coupe. Though fundamentally unchanged for 1978, it gained a new nose section and new rear bumpers. While the standard engine was still the in-line six-cylinder 250cu in unit, both 305 and 350cu in V8s were also available to pep up the performance.

234

Above: 1978 Oldsmobile Starfire GT Coupe. The Starfire was little changed for 1978 but a GT option was introduced. It had a 231cu in V6 engine, special GT stripes, rally wheels, and special raised white lettering tires.

Left: 1978 Chevrolet Corvette Coupe. Big news at Corvette was at the rear of the car in 1978, when a wraparound rear window was added to improve the aerodynamics as part of the Corvette's 25th anniversary package. Removeable glass roof panels were also now available. The higher performance L82 engine option was tweaked to push the power output up to 220hp, and a special edition Indy Pace Car replica was offered at $13,653, a considerable premium over the standard $9,446 sticker price.

Right: 1978 Oldsmobile Cutlass Coupe. The Oldsmobile Cutlass was part of the 1978 down-sizing regime. Eight models were offered in all, with different styles of grille. The Cutlass Calais was built on a Supreme body, but had its own unique wrapover vertical eggcrate-style grille.

Below Right: 1978 Buick Regal Turbo Sport Coupe. While before Regal had been part of the Century line-up, in 1978 it became a separate line in its own right. Three versions were offered: the V6 Regal two-door coupe, V6 Turbo Regal Sport, and V6 or V8 Regal Limited. The new Regal had also been down-sized considerably — it was now some 14in shorter than before.

Far Right, Top: 1978 Buick Skyhawk Hatchback. The sub-compact Buick Skyhawk hatchback, fitted with the 231cu in 105hp V6, continued largely unchanged in 1978. Total production that year was only 24,500 units, perhaps because its $4,103 sticker price was undercut by both the Skylark S at $3,872 and by the base Skylark at $3,999.

Far Right, Bottom: 1978 Buick Century Special. Yet another victim of the relentless down-sizing campaign of the late 1970s, the 1978 Buick Century was both 10in shorter and some 600lb lighter than before. Two-door coupe, four-door sedan, and four-door station wagons were available

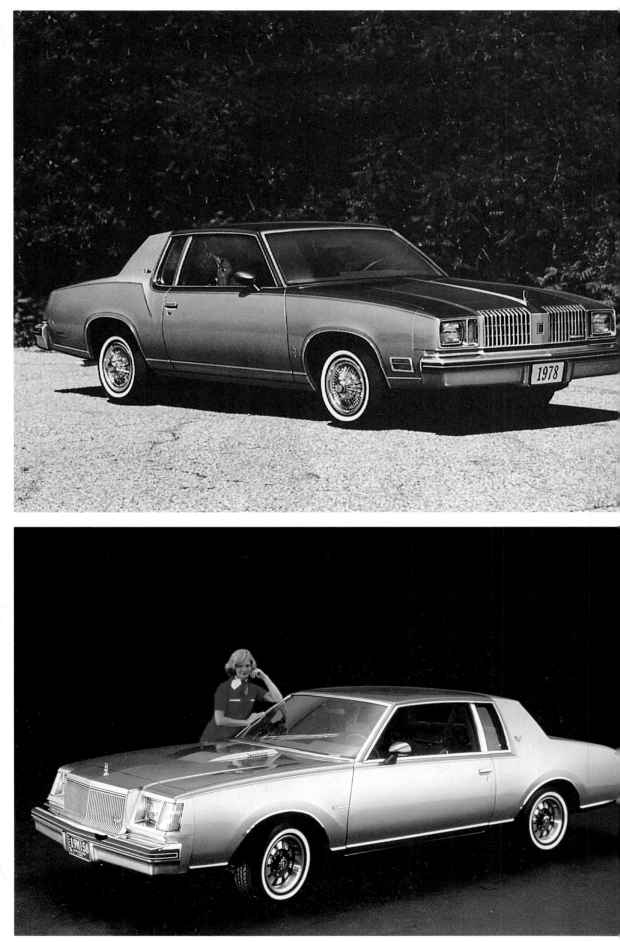

Right: Most of the changes to the Ford Mustang in 1978 revolved around the interior trims and new colors. A new electronic voltage regulator gave a longer-life reliability guarantee than the previous electro-mechanical version. A variable-ratio power steering option was also added.

Below: 1978 Pontiac Sunbird Formula Hatchback Coupe. Pontiac's entry-level sub-compact Sunbird had a sticker price starting at only $2,662. The range consisted of two-door coupe, two-door hatch coupe, two-door sport coupe, and two-door station wagon.

238

Above: 1978 Ford Fairmont Futura. The Fairmont range replaced the Maverick as the company's compact offering. Styled by Ghia in Italy, the original line-up consisted of just sedan and station wagon. However, the Sport Coupe was launched in December 1978 to boost the range with a distinctive looking two-door coupe.

Left: 1978 Ford Thunderbird. The biggest news for Thunderbird in 1978 was Ford's 75th anniversary. A limited Diamond Jubilee edition was launched — luxuriously designed inside and out. The regular Thunderbirds had six new body colors and four vinyl roof colors.

1 9 7 0 s

Above: 1978 Lincoln Continental Mk V Coupe. Basically unchanged from previous years, the 1978 Mk V Coupe line-up gained a Diamond Jubilee special edition in blue or gold metallic paintwork, and a unique Valino grain landau roof and matching Valino grain molding. Cost was a mere $8,000 — to be added to the sticker price of the standard Mk V, which added another $12,099 to the bottom line.

Right: 1979 Cadillac Eldorado Coupe. The inevitable happened in 1979, and the Eldorado was down-sized and lost 20in overall. Interior space, however, was uncompromised. It was also given independent rear suspension for a smoother ride. As was the Cadillac norm, numerous special editions were also produced, from the Seville d'Elegance to the DeVille Custom Phantom.

Left: 1979 Buick Electra Park Avenue Sedan. Four rectangular headlights and a new grille gave the 1979 Electra a new appearance. During the year over 120,000 Electras were sold, including 44,000 of the most expensive Park Avenue derivatives — despite a price hike that took the Electra Park Avenue sedan's sticker price up from $8,598 to $9,959.

Below: 1979 Buick Riviera Coupe. Down-sized and also re-engineered for front-wheel drive, the new Riviera retained the 350cu in V8 from before, but a special Riviera S Type was also available fitted with a 231cu in turbocharged V6 producing 185hp. At the time this was the only American front-wheel drive car fitted with a turbocharged engine.

Right: 1979 Pontiac Firebird Formula. No great changes were made to 1979 Pontiacs, except for some engine revision, particularly for cars destined for sale in California. The Firebird range did see new quad headlamp designs and the eradication of a grille. The Firebird Formula's standard engine was a 301cu in V8 pushing out 150hp.

Below: 1979 Buick LeSabre Sport Coupe. A restyled front and rear end freshened the LeSabre range for 1979. The Sport Coupe, powered by Buick's 231cu in V6 Turbo, produced 170hp and cost $6,621 at the time, a modest $500 more than the standard LeSabre coupe, despite the fact that the Sport was fitted not only with the more powerful turbo engine, but also with uprated springs and dampers, chrome wheels and wider tyres and a revised sporty steering rack.

Above, Left and Below Left: 1979 Oldsmobile Hurst/Olds. By way of a change, Oldsmobile brought out a Hurst/Olds option on the Cutlass Calais in 1979. It had a 5.7-liter four-barrel V8 engine and automatic transmission. The paint options were a splendid black and gold or white and gold with gold aluminum sport wheel and mirrors. Under 3,000 were built.

Above: 1979 Chevrolet Caprice Classic. A new grille, bigger fenders, and wider three-lamp tail-light clusters distinguished the 1979 Chevrolet Caprice from the $300 cheaper Impala range. As before, two-door sport coupe and landau coupe, four-door sedan, and four- door station wagon derivatives were available.

Right: 1979 Ford Mustang. The Mustang got a new look for 1979, provided by an all new sheetmetal body. Its chassis was shortened and modified to hold the new body metal, which wiped out the familiar curved crease in the bodyside. Just as most cars were shrinking, the Mustang grew longer, and got more passenger space.

Above: 1979 AMC Pacer. AMC had first introduced the Pacer at the Chicago Auto Show in 1975. At the time it was the first completely new car that AMC had launched for many years, and it certainly did not go unnoticed, thanks to its unique hatchback body with a high glass area and sloping hood.

Left: 1979 Pontiac Grand Am Sport Coupe. Though the standard Pontiac Firebird Grand Am had a sticker price of $6,299, for 1979 a special edition was produced at a lofty $10,620 — a considerable premium. It was fitted with a 220hp V8 in place of the standard Grand Am's 185hp unit and also enjoyed a host of technical and comfort items. Total Grand Am production topped the 117,000 mark this year.

Above: 1979 Lincoln Collectors Series Sedan. Intended to be the most prestigious Continental of them all, the Collectors Series Sedan was identified by its paintwork — only white and midnight blue metallic paint options were available, and in both cases the roof was also body paint colored. The sticker price of the Collectors Series Sedan could comfortably exceed the $20,000 barrier.

Right: 1979 Ford LTD II. Not one of Ford's greatest successes, the LTD II would be phased out at the end of 1979. The 400cu in option was deleted, leaving a choice between the standard 302cu in V8 and the optional 351cu in. Ford also offered an optional larger fuel tank in tacit acceptance of the LTD II's poor fuel consumption.

Above: 1979 Pontiac Firebird Esprit Redbird. All it took to really get noticed in 1979 was the $449 it cost to specify the aggressive Redbird appearance package on the Pontiac Firebird Esprit.

Left: 1979 Ford Thunderbird. The Limited edition Thunderbird was continued in 1979 as the Heritage. The standard Thunderbird had a bolder, heavier-looking grille and a new spoiler. The flight bench was now standard seating, covered with Rosano cloth and with fold-down armrests.

248

Above: 1979 Chevrolet Monza 2+2 Spyder Sport. More horses under the hood was the Chevrolet Monza story for 1979. The base 151cu in four-cylinder engine now produced 90hp while 192 and 231cu in V6s or a 305cu in V8 were also available — the latter producing a maximum of 130hp.

Left: 1979 Pontiac Trans Am 10th Anniversary. In 1979 it cost $449 to specify the aggressive Redbird appearance package on the Pontiac Firebird Esprit. A limited edition Trans Am 10th Anniversary package was also available.

The 1980s

Chrysler was not alone in struggling financially as the 1970s rolled over into the 1980s. President Jimmy Carter and the federal government had literally saved Chrysler's life by agreeing to guarantee loans of up to $1.5 billion — $800 million of which Chrysler needed in the first year alone.

At the same time, Ford's share price fell to its lowest for years and American Motors was forced to tie up with Renault of France in order to stay in business — the first time that control of a US car company had fallen into foreign ownership.

During 1980, new car sales dropped to below the nine million mark and imports from Japan continued to increase at ever quicker pace. The Detroit motor industry started losing money like water — $4.2 billion in that one year alone.

Unions tried to encourage patriotic Americans to 'Buy American' and Ford petitioned the International Trade Commission to impose strict quotas on the Japanese car makers, but the request was turned down in the name of free trade. There was also the important question of consumer choice; what the American auto makers could not deny was that great numbers of US

citizens preferred the smaller and vastly more reliable and economical Japanese imports. Their choice in the showrooms was clear — and in 1980 Japanese cars claimed over 21% of the total market.

Chrysler may have looked close to dead and buried in 1980, but Chairman Lee Iacocca quickly got to work turning the company round. He cut costs, reduced his own salary, persuaded Chrysler's workers to forego pay and benefits, and — his most significant move of all — sanctioned the introduction of the Chrysler minivan. This was to be a model that would not only ensure the company's survival, but would also change the whole face of American family transport.

Iacocca's efforts quickly took effect and he was able to stage-manage the return of over $800 million of the federal loans in late 1983 — which was seven years earlier than was required by the loan agreement.

1983 saw the start of recovery from recession for all US auto makers. While sales had dropped to under eight million in 1982, they recovered to just over nine million the following year.

And in 1984, Ford, Chrysler, and GM all reported record profits, while struggling AMC also saw its figures change from red to black. Sales rose again, to 10.3 million in 1984, 11 million the following year and then to an all-time record in 1986 — 11.4 million units.

Chrysler's profits continued to rise and Lee Iacocca became something of a national hero, for rescuing the company from bankruptcy, then getting involved in the restoration of the Statue of Liberty which, like Chrysler itself, had

Right: 1980 Buick Skylark Sedan. The new Skylark was the first Buick car of the 1980s and was a version of the relatively unpopular X-car and a cousin of the Chevrolet Citation. It was front-drive and had an all new unibody chassis. It weighed around 800lb less than the previous Skylark and was much more fuel-efficient.

fallen into poor repair as a result of neglect over many years.

AMC, however, was still struggling despite Renault's best efforts, and was still far from healthy. In 1987, it was bought by Chrysler for $2 billion and for that Chrysler gained not only the famous Jeep marque, but also AMC's car ranges and all its factories and production plants in the USA and Canada.

The Japanese, meanwhile, were still making steady progress too. As domestic complaints continued to be heard that the Japanese were dumping cars in the US market in order to buy market share, President Ronald Reagan's administration brokered a deal under which the Japanese agreed to a voluntary limit to their US exports. The limit was set at 1.68 million cars for 1981, a small but significant reduction on the numbers they had exported the previous year. Frustrated in their efforts to export more, the Japanese changed tack and started investing in their own 'transplant' manufacturing complexes.

Honda began building cars at a greenfield site in Maryland in 1982. Mazda, Nissan, Toyota, and Mitsubishi all followed suit. To quell the continuing disquiet of the US auto makers and the unions, the Japanese agreed to extend the voluntary restrictions on exports until 1985, by which time the limit had reached 2.4 million.

The appetite of the American car-buying public for Japanese cars was still not satisfied, and at last the Big Three US auto makers began to respond positively to the threat, recognizing that Japan's success had less to do with dumping and unfair trade, and far more to do with product quality, manufacturing excellence, and sheer industrial efficiency.

GM set the ball rolling with its announcement of the establishment of an all-new division — Saturn. Its task would be to design and build a compact line of cars for the US market. Crucially, the new division would not be located in Detroit but, like the Japanese transplants, would take advantage of a brand new greenfield site on which a world-class manufacturing plant could be built with the express aim of producing cars to the quality and efficiency standards of the very best of the Japanese.

It remains to be seen whether Saturn will turn out to be too little, too late, because as the 1980s progressed, the progress being made by the Japanese — and later the Koreans too — seemed unstoppable.

In the last few years of the decade, Toyota launched its upmarket Lexus brand, Nissan its Infiniti brand, and Honda its Acura brand. After years of selling compact cars, the Japanese were now competing head on with Detroit's larger luxury cars.

Subaru and Isuzu opened a plant in Lafayette to build light trucks and cars, Honda expanded its Marysville plant to add the Civic to its output, and Hyundai started low-cost exports, selling nearly 170,000 units in its first year, against a target of only 100,000.

By the end of the decade, there were 11 Japanese transplant operations up and running in North America, all of which had been conceived, planned, and brought into production since Honda's groundbreaking move just eight years earlier.

Not only had the Japanese taken over 33% of the American market by 1989, but they were now selling some 3.28 million cars a year — 780,000 of them actually built in the USA.

Perhaps more frightening still for the Big Three was the fact that in that last year of the decade, the Honda Accord only failed to become the highest-selling car in the USA by a mere 4,000 units. It would not be long before its knocked the Ford Escort off its number one spot.

Below: 1980 Buick Electra Estate Wagon. Streamlining was the Buick buzz word for 1980. Even its station wagon began to look dynamic. A new grille, sloping fenders, and a 200lb curb weight loss all helped enhance the Electra Estate Wagon's appearance.

Right: 1980 Buick Century Sport Aero Coupe. Buick's Century model had spent two years with a slantback roof and now, in 1980, a notchback sedan roofline was introduced on two-door Century models. Sport and Turbo coupe options had black trims and a hawk decal on the front fender.

Below 1980 Oldsmobile Cutlass Salon Slantback. By 1980, there were 10 Cutlass models on the market — including three notchback sedans which were brand new. Each side of the Salon's grille had a series of horizontal bars with a further three vertical bars on top. Oldsmobile continued the slantback styling on the Salon coupe.

Above: 1980 Chevrolet Citation. The Citation was rather strangely billed by Chevrolet as the 'most thoroughly tested new car in Chevy history.' Unfortunately, this new X-car, Chevrolet's first front drive vehicle was charged with having seriously flawed brakes — an issue that was never completely resolved. Initially, however, this functional family-size car sold very well.

Left: 1980 Chevrolet Camaro Berlinetta Coupe. The Berlinetta had replaced the Type LT in Chevrolet's Camaro range in 1979 and a year later, it was still doing well. The coupe had white-wall tires, bright headlamp bezels, sport mirrors, and wire wheel covers.

Left: 1980 Ford Thunderbird. The Ford Thunderbird celebrated its 25th anniversary in 1980, and gained a new body and a new engine. It was lighter than before, and this ninth generation model was now designed to hold only four passengers, not six. All Silver Anniversary models had Dove Grey interiors and automatic overdrive transmission as standard.

Below Left: 1980 Checker Taxi. The evergreen Checker taxi continued to be the mainstay of the New York cab fleet during the 1980s. Even then, passengers often found drivers unable to find their way to the city's most famous landmarks and incapable of understanding basic English. But at least their Checkers were reliable.

Far Left, Top: 1980 Chevrolet Monte Carlo. Chevrolet changed the Monte Carlo's headlamps in 1980. New quad rectangular headlamps were placed above wide rectangular parking lamps. Horizontal lenses ahead of the wheel replaced the wrap around side marker lamps. The new base engine became the 3.8-liter V6.

Far Left, Bottom: 1980 Mustang Cobra Turbo. Ford Mustang's sporty little Cobra model got a new look to its front and rear in 1980. It had been restyled with the 1979 Indy Pace Car in mind. The modern Mustang, which had been down-sized the previous year fitted in with the 1980 economy ethos at Ford.

Above: 1980 Ford Pinto. 1980 was the last year Ford would produce the Pinto — it had already waved good-bye to the down-sized LTD II. All models this year had four-cylinder engines, the once optional V6 having been phased out. The Pinto was to be replaced by the new front-drive Escort.

Right: 1981 Chevrolet Malibu Classic. Chevrolet's mid-size Malibu got a minor makeover in 1981. The four-door sedan was given a squarish formal roofline and a new back window section, which drew comparisons with Buick's 1980 Century. Classic models had a stand-up hood ornament and came in a variety of bespoke colors.

Above: 1981 Oldsmobile 98 Regency Sedan. The Regency was the top 98 that Oldsmobile offered in 1981. Coupe and sedan versions were available, and a few dollars more bought a digital clock and opera lamps, on top of the standard 4.1-liter V8 engine and four-speed automatic overdrive transmission.

Left: 1981 Chevrolet Chevette. Chevrolet claimed that its Chevette was America's most popular subcompact. Whether or not that was strictly true, the Chevette got a new flush-mounted windscreen with black outline molding. It certainly wasn't the fastest subcompact, with its 1.6-liter engine mated to a four-speed manual transmission.

Above: 1981 Buick Regal Ltd. Buick revamped the Regal in 1981, releasing it from the doldrums of down-sized coupe land. It was now seriously aerodynamic with a raked down front end and spoiler type cut off. A turbo edition and 4.3-liter V8 options were added to the standard V6 engine.

Right: 1981 Oldsmobile Cutlass Calais T-Top Saloon. Oldsmobile customers had to face large price rises again in 1981, but they were offered a large range in return. The Cutlass series had eight models. The standard engine offered was a 3.8-liter V6 with column-shift automatic transmission and power brakes. The Calais had specially painted wheel covers and front and rear stabilizer bars.

Above: 1981 Dodge Omni 24. Dodge, like almost every other manufacturer, was promoting fuel economy in 1981. Though there were no major revisions to the Omni this year, the 024 coupe was no longer listed in the same catalogue as the sedan, although it remained part of the family.

Left: 1981 Cadillac Fleetwood Brougham. In 1981, Cadillac's flagship model was again the Fleetwood Brougham. Available as coupe and sedan, the Broughams shared several features with the DeVilles but there was no mistaking the two. The Brougham, touted as the 'Cadillac of Cadillacs' was the infinitely superior model.

Right: 1981 Ford Thunderbird. The Thunderbird provided customers with a shock in 1981. The V8 had been replaced by a six-cylinder in-line engine as standard. To make up for that, many of the goodies previously available only on the luxury models were now being offered on all models. One interesting new option was self-sealing puncture-resistant tyres.

Below Right: 1981 Ford Mustang. In 1981, the Ford Mustang was given a variety of manual transmission ratios, both four-speed and a new five-speed. Joining the option list was a T-roof with twin removable tinted-glass panels, which was available on the two-door notchback or three-door hatchback.

Bottom Right: 1983 Ford Thunderbird. The tenth-generation Thunderbird appeared in 1983, with a smaller, more aerodynamic form. This new Thunderbird was aimed at the younger market, and a turbo coupe was also produced. The turbocharger in this design was specifically positioned to provide faster response times and reduce turbo lag.

Left: 1982 Ford Mustang.
1982 saw the return of the
Mustang 5.0-liter Sport
Option Coupe. Performance-
orientated Mustangs were
again available with a high-
output engine and four-speed
manual overdrive transmission, a combination last
offered in 1979. Thanks to a
new, larger exhaust system
the 1982 Mustang delivered
much faster acceleration than
the 1979 model.

Below Left: 1984 Ford
Thunderbird. Although the
1984 Thunderbird had few
exterior alterations, the
model line-up was revised.
Heritage became Elan, and a
Fila edition was introduced
in conjunction with Fila
Sports, the Italian sportswear
manufacturer.

Bottom Left: The 1983
Mustang model was more or
less a carry-over from the
year before. It did, however,
have a restyled nose and rear
end which improved its aerodynamics. The new angled
front had deeply recessed
headlight housings with the
Ford Oval placed at the centre of a narrower grille design
that tapered inward slightly at
the base.

Above: 1981 Chevrolet Camaro. The Rally Sport was dropped from the Camaro line up in 1981, which left the Sport Coupe, the Berlinetta, and the performance Z28. The Z28 had a standard four-barrel V8 engine, with new wide ratio four-speed manual transmission. It also sported a front air dam, front fender flares, and hood scoop with decal.

Right: 1981 Ford Ltd Crown Victoria. Ford's range of full size cars, the LTDs, had lost their standard full-size engine by 1981. Instead, they were fitted with 4.2-liter V8 engines, with automatic overdrive transmission. The three speed automatic had been dropped. Unfortunately, the smaller base powerplant didn't do much to improve mpg.

Left: 1981 Ford Escort Wagon. Ford introduced the brand new front-wheel drive Escort 'world car' in 1981. It had been designed to capture a part of the subcompact market for Ford. The wagons had less-sloped rear windows and vertical wraparound tail lights.

Below: 1981 Ford Granada Coupe. Ford was only going to allow the Granada another two years of life after 1981, but it got a dynamic restyle in this year nevertheless. According to Ford, in fact, it was 'the industry's most changed American-built sedan for 1981.' Despite having shrunk by 3in, the Granada was, in fact, roomier than ever inside and it also offered more luggage space.

Far Left: 1982 Pontiac Firebird. Pontiac knocked one model off its Firebird range in 1982, leaving revised base, luxury SE, and Trans Am options. Each had its own suspension and tire setup. The electrically controlled halogen headlamps were hidden in the low nose, and park/signal lamps sat in slots inboard of the headlamps.

Left: The 1982 Buick Riviera Convertible was the first Buick ragtop since 1975. It was an historic occasion and signaled the start of a new trend for open-top cars.

Below: The 1982 Buick Skyhawk Sedan was styled along the lines of the Century, using the GM J-car platform. It had front-wheel drive, a 2.0-liter engine, and MacPherson independent front suspension. It was offered in Custom and Limited trim levels, available on either coupe or sedan bodies.

Above: 1982 Chevrolet Cavalier. The Cavalier was a new introduction to the Chevrolet line in 1982. It was hopefully marketed as a subcompact outside, but with the space of a compact inside. Four models of Cavalier were offered; two- and four-door sedans, two-door hatchback, and four-door wagon. The only engine available to begin with was a 1.8-liter unit.

Left: 1982 DeLorean. At the time, the 1982 gull-winged DeLorean sports car looked stunning with its stainless steel finish, but the unsavory fact was that the Renault V6-powered car was ill-conceived and poorly built and the company itself was underfunded despite massive grants from the UK Government to ensure the DeLorean was manufactured in Northern Ireland. Later DeLoreans benefited from a Lotus-tuned suspension set-up that improved matters no end, but by then potential customers had lost faith in the marque. Receivers took over the business and the police were called in to assess whether fraud had been committed in the running of the short-lived business. The end result is a handful of cars in collector's hands that are now little more than a historical oddity.

Above: 1982 Chevrolet Camaro Z28 Coupe. The Camaro's fastback profile included a compound S-shaped glass hatch. The Z28's front end had no upper grille opening, while 'ground effect' air dams reached lower towards the ground. The Z28 was also fitted with special aluminum wheels.

Right: 1982 Cadillac Cimarron. To compete with European manufacturers, Cadillac brought out the Cimarron, a small luxury car in 1982. It was given the first four-cylinder engine Cadillac had used since 1914 and the first manual shift since 1953. To prove it was still a luxury vehicle despite its dimensions, even the trunk was carpeted and nine hand-buffed body colors were available.

Left: 1982 Ford Exp Sport Coupe. Ford introduced the Exp in 1982. It was the first new two-seater to grace the Ford range in 25 years. It wasn't intended, however, to follow in the footsteps of the Thunderbird. It was going to be radically different in fact; very affordable, and very fuel efficient. The Exp also weighed an astonishing thousand pounds less than the Thunderbird.

Below: 1982 Mercury Lynx Villager Wagon. Lynx had become Mercury's best selling line by 1982. A new five-door hatchback model had been added to the original two-door hatchback and four-door wagon. That was the only major change to the line as the Lynx's appearance was left unaltered in this year.

Above: 1982 Ford Fairmount Futura. Ford tagged on 'Futura' to the Fairmount name in 1982. It also reduced the line-up to a single series. Fairmounts continued to be used as taxis and police cars, the 4.2-liter V8 being available only to these models. The Fairmount had also been given a new front end.

Right: 1982 Chevrolet Corvette. For the first time since 1955, no stick shift Corvettes were produced. Every one had a four-speed automatic, with lock up in every gear except first. 1982 also saw the first fuel-injected Corvette in nearly two decades. Externally, this final version of the big Corvettes was pretty much unaltered.

Above: 1982 Buick Regal Ltd Sedan. 1982 was the first year that the Regal line included a four-door sedan or estate wagon. It was Buick's last remaining rear-wheel drive mid-size range. Regal Limiteds were available with automatic door locks and Gran Touring suspension.

Left: 1983 Pontiac Fiero. Launched in late 1983 as an 84 model, the plastic-bodied Pontiac Fiero was a new sort of American sports car — one that offered pretty good performance but good levels of fuel economy too. According to Pontiac's figures, the Fiero was good for 0-60mph acceleration in 12.5 seconds — or 11.5 seconds with the optional 4.10:1 rear axle — but at the same time it offered an EPA mileage figure of 27 mpg in the city and an astonishing 47 mpg on the highway.

Right: 1983 Chevrolet Monte Carlo SS. The Monte Carlo SS joined the Chevrolet range in 1983, a significant improvement on the base model, with its high output version of Chevy's carbureted 305cu in V8. Interest in rear-drive mid-size vehicles revived in this year, and the Monte Carlo was a popular choice, a coupe able to carry six people quite comfortably.

Below: 1983 Chevrolet Celebrity. The luxury aerodynamic five-passenger Chevrolet Celebrity was offered with a diesel V6 engine option for the first time in 1983. It was Chevrolet's biggest front-wheel drive, available with a 2.5-liter fuel-injected four-cylinder engine, an optional 2.8-liter gas V6 and the diesel. Ten body colors were offered.

Above: 1983 Buick Skylark Coupe T-Type. Although the Skylark was basically the Buick economy range, this wasn't a point Buick liked to linger on. It preferred the word compact. The T Type was a new Skylark, with stylish black trim, a 2.8-liter V6 engine, manual four-speed gearbox, and specially tuned exhaust. It also had the widest wheels of any Buick T Type.

Left: 1983 Buick Skyhawk Wagon. The Skyhawk station wagon was a new addition to Buick's family in 1983, and was the first front-wheel drive Buick wagon. It was available with both Custom and Limited trim and had a cargo volume of 64.5cu ft.

Above: 1983 Cadillac Seville. By 1983, the Seville was awash with nice little touches from reminder chimes to overhead assist handles. The full cabriolet roof that simulated a convertible top was available in four colors. A new sound system was also available with Dolby tape noise reduction.

Right: 1983 Cadillac Cimarron. After its innovations the previous year, 1983 was a modest one for Cadillac. Cimarron sales were still unimpressive despite the introduction of a special edition. The other lines, however, were as popular as ever.

Left: 1983 Mercury Topaz. Mercury replaced the Zephyr with the brand new front drive Topaz in 1983. The Topaz sold well right from the start, due in part to Hertz buying over 15,000 of them for its rental fleet. The Topaz was closely linked to the Tempo and was built on a stretched Lynx platform.

Below: The Cadillac Seville Cabriolet Sedan underwent some minor modifications, such as restyled taillamps, which gave it a slightly fresher look for 1984, but overall, this was a quiet year for Cadillac.

Above: 1984 Pontiac Fiero. In its early days, the Pontiac Fiero sold well and contributed to the best Pontiac sales' year so far this decade. The first compact mid-engined sports car to be offered in America, the Fiero was fitted with a 151cu in four-cylinder engine producing a relatively modest 92hp. But what it lacked in sheer performance, it more than made up for in terms of looks.

Right: 1984 Cadillac Eldorado Biarritz Convertible. This was the first year since 1976 that Cadillac had produced a convertible — the elegant Eldorado Biarritz. In a particularly pleasing piece of technological innovation, its rear and side windows raised and lowered automatically with the power top and it featured a glass back window. Convertibles had specific door and fender accent moldings and Biarritz script nameplate.

Left: 1984 Buick Century Custom Wagon. The Buick Century range offered two new wagons in 1984, the Custom and the Estate. They both had a top hinged tailgate and split-folding back seat. They were produced to replace the now defunct Regal rear-drive wagon, and could hold around 74cu ft of cargo.

Below: The Buick Riviera T Type Coupe was the recipient of a number of modifications in 1984. It got a new turbocharged 3.8-liter V6 engine, as well as an LED tachometer and a leather-wrapped steering wheel.

Right: 1984 Oldsmobile Firenza GT Hatchback. Oldsmobile was aiming the Firenza at the younger market, playing on its sporty qualities and dynamic design. The GT's front was updated in 1984 and other colors were now made available in addition to the original red. Poly-cast sport wheels and black accents were also now included in the specification.

Below: 1984 Oldsmobile Cutlass Ciera. Oldsmobile updated the Cutlass Ciera's front and rear for 1984. The twin sections of this year's grille now consisted of thin vertical bars. Each model could seat six people and had divided bench and custom seats.

Left: 1984 Pontiac Trans Am Grand Prix Pace Car. Extensive wind tunnel testing had resulted in a new and more aerodynamic style for the Firebirds from 1982, but it remained important to stress the Trans Am's impeccable performance credentials too. So for 1984, Pontiac ensured the Trans Am was used as Pace Car at important race meetings — providing plenty of publicity and reinforcing the performance car image at the same time.

Below Left: 1984 Lincoln Continental Mk VII. Lincoln decided to be dramatic in 1984, and described the new Mark VII as 'the most airflow efficient luxury car built in America' thanks to its drag coefficient at 0.38.

Above: 1984 Ford Exp Turbo Coupe. Ford's Exp was made even more desirable in 1984 with the addition of a turbocharger. The turbo model had a front air dam, rear decklid spoiler, and 'turbo' decals at strategic points to single it out from the other Exp's. The turbo package also came with harder suspension, new shock absorbers, and five-speed manual transaxle.

Right: 1984 Ford Tempo. The front-drive Ford Tempo was a replacement for the Fairmount, which had been rear-wheel drive. The Mercury Topaz was almost identical but with different trim and options available. The Tempo had a factory-installed anti-theft system, remote release fuel filler door, and looked like a jelly bean.

Left: The 1984 Lincoln Continental Town Car. The 1984 Lincoln Continental Town Car had the longest wheelbase of Cadillac's sedan range. It was almost unaltered from the year before, but 1984 saw the introduction of the town car signature series and the Cartier Designer series.

Below: 1985 Pontiac Grand Prix. Pontiac's 1985 six-seater Grand Prix sedan was similar in appearance to the 1983 and 1984 models though it varied in trim details. Power for standard models came from a 231cu in V6 producing 110hp, though a 350cu in V8 diesel producing 105hp could also be specified.

Right: 1985 Oldsmobile
Cutlass Supreme. The 4-4-2
package replaced the two-
year old Hurst/Olds option in
1985 in the Oldsmobile
Cutlass Supreme line. This
new version had a powerful
V8 and reworked suspension.
Sedan grilles now had thin
horizontal strips divided into
four sections.

Below Right: 1985 Pontiac
Parisienne Brougham Sedan.
At $11,125 sticker price, the
1985 Pontiac Parisienne
Brougham Sedan was the
flagship of the Parisienne
range. Engine options available were 231cu in V6,
305cu in V8 petrol, and
350cu in V8 diesel.

Left: 1985 Buick Electra Sedan. The Buick Electra that appeared in 1985 was an entirely new one. Although it had lost huge chunks of its exterior and its weight, internal dimensions were reasonably unaffected. These cuts made it 2ft shorter, 4in narrower and 600lb lighter than the previous model. A coupe and sedan were available in both plush Park Avenue and original base form.

Below Left: 1985 Buick Grand National.

Right: 1985 Buick Regal Grand National Coupe. The Grand National was Buick Regal's performance edition, which became available in 1985. Offered only in stylish black, it was marketed at younger buyers, which signaled the beginning of an image change for Buick. The Grand National could do 0-60 in eight seconds.

Below: The 1985 Buick Electra Estate Wagon was the classier of Buick's two station wagons. It continued with rear-wheel drive, despite the alterations made on the coupe and sedan ranges. Two and three rows of seats were available.

Above: 1985 Buick Somerset Regal Limited Coupe. Yuppies and baby boomers were given another car to choose from in 1985, when Buick launched the Somerset Regal series. This personal luxury sport coupe replaced the X-body Skylark. The limited edition came complete with chrome bumpers, woodgrain instrument panel, and wheel opening moldings.

Left: 1985 Cadillac Seville Elegante Sedan. Cadillacs became front-wheel drive in 1985 and with this change the 1985 DeVille and Fleetwood both lost two feet in length. The Brougham, however, continued with rear-wheel drive which did nothing to harm its popularity. This was the Seville's last season in this design.

Right: 1985 Oldsmobile Firenza Cruiser. The Firenza Cruiser was Oldsmobile's 1985 subcompact station wagon, available in base or LX trim versions. For this year a new Chevrolet 173cu in V6 was offered as an alternative to the standard 2.0-liter four-cylinder unit.

Below: 1985 Mercury Marquis. The Marquis was almost identical to the Ford LTD. It was a mid-size rear-drive and had been redesigned in 1983, using the former Cougar platform. A high performance V8 option was planned: it would have been similar to the Ford LTD LX model, but it failed to materialize. The Brougham was the top of the range Marquis.

Left: 1985 Mustang. Ragtop mechanical components and a new front end were the focus of changes to the Mustang in 1985. A four-hole integral air dam appeared below the bumper, between the parking lights. Both notch-back and hatchback body options continued. The GT option was cheap to run, performed better than the turbo under normal conditions but could still deliver excellent performance.

Below: 1985 Mercury Cougar XR-7 Coupe. Mercury gave the Cougar a mini makeover in 1985. Its grille now looked rather Mercedes-esque, but its basic body shape was unaltered. The XR-7 came with a turbocharged four with five-speed gearbox and performance Goodyear Gator tires on cast aluminum wheels.

Right and Below: 1986 Cadillac Seville Elegante (Right) and Eldorado (Below). The 1986 Cadillac restyle of these models surprised customers by the similarities between the two. Both were fitted with impressive electronic instruments. The Seville lost 17in and 375lb in its makeover, as well as the more distinctive elements of its style.

Far Right, Top: 1986 Buick LeSabre Ltd Coupe. Buick's increasingly aerodynamic designs were typified by the LeSabre's 1986. With transverse-mounted engine and front-wheel drive, it was available as fastback coupe or notchback sedan and with Custom or Limited trim.

Far Right, Bottom: The Buick Century Custom Sedan received a new look in 1986, with a remodeling of its front end. The vertical element grille was slanted and protruded below the headlamps, continuing around the edges of the front fenders.

Above: 1986 Buick Riviera. 1986 saw the Buick Riviera's first restyle in seven years. While its front-wheel drive and fully independent suspension remained, the rest was brand new. Smaller, lighter, and aerodynamically improved, its 3.8 V6 engine now produced 140hp.

Right: The 1986 Buick Skyhawk had flush-mounted glass, integrated bumpers, and styled mirrors. Several models were available from the high performing Sport/Hatch and T Type to the more sedate Custom and Limited.

Far Right, Top: The 1986 Chevrolet Corvette Indy Pace Car was bright yellow and styled like the new convertible with special track lights. All Convertibles were called pace cars as that seemed to mean 'open top' to Chevrolet.

Far Right, Bottom: The 1986 Chevrolet Nova was the result of a joint venture between Toyota and Chevrolet and appeared in 1986. Originally a four-door hatchback, a four-door notch-back was added to the range soon after its launch. It could seat five people.

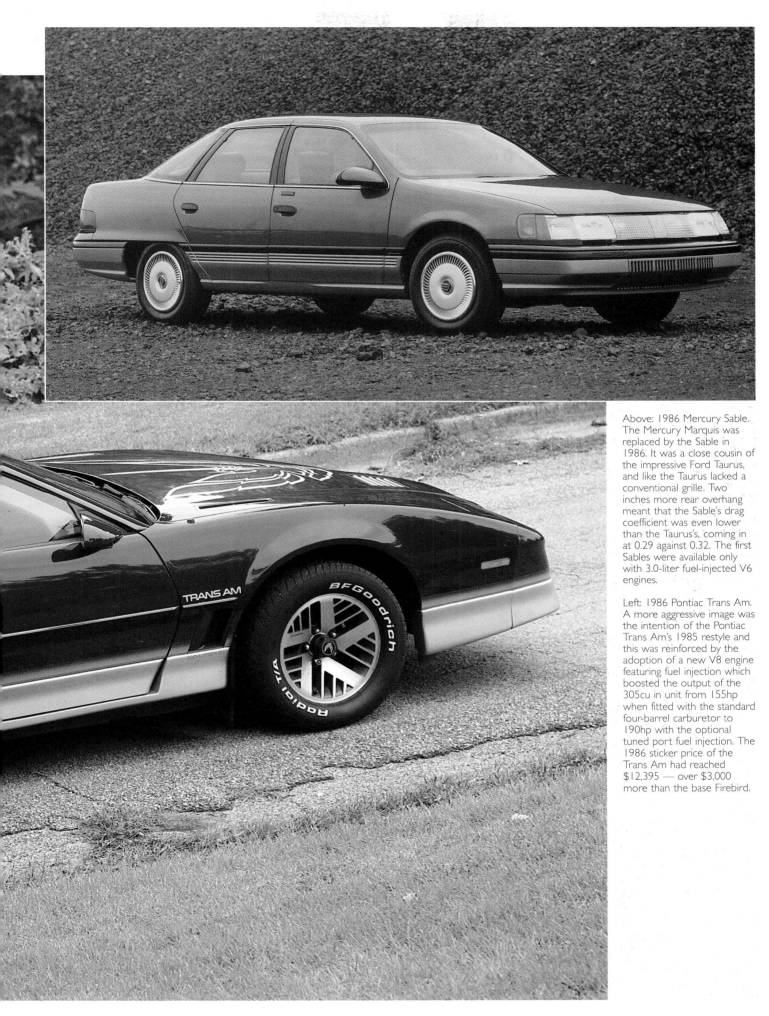

Above: 1986 Mercury Sable. The Mercury Marquis was replaced by the Sable in 1986. It was a close cousin of the impressive Ford Taurus, and like the Taurus lacked a conventional grille. Two inches more rear overhang meant that the Sable's drag coefficient was even lower than the Taurus's, coming in at 0.29 against 0.32. The first Sables were available only with 3.0-liter fuel-injected V6 engines.

Left: 1986 Pontiac Trans Am. A more aggressive image was the intention of the Pontiac Trans Am's 1985 restyle and this was reinforced by the adoption of a new V8 engine featuring fuel injection which boosted the output of the 305cu in unit from 155hp when fitted with the standard four-barrel carburetor to 190hp with the optional tuned port fuel injection. The 1986 sticker price of the Trans Am had reached $12,395 — over $3,000 more than the base Firebird.

296

Left: 1987 Ford Thunderbird. New in the Ford camp for 1987 was a 5.0-liter Thunderbird Sport model. The rest of the range got all-new sheet metal and aero-style headlamps. To make room for the new sports model, the Elan was renamed the LX.

Below Left: The lucky 1987 Dodge Lancer got a rear window defogger as standard in 1987. Both the base and the ES were available with 146hp turbocharged engines. The Lancer Shelby also became a model in its own right this year, having been introduced initially only in small quantities.

Far Left, Top: 1986 Ford Taurus Wagon. With no grille at the front and a wide rounded rear glass area at the back, the 1986 Ford Taurus Wagon was distinctive in styling. Under the skin it shared much of its drivetrain and transmissions with the Sable. The Wagons could be specified with a rear facing third seat and folding load floor extension that could also serve as a picnic table.

Far Left, Bottom: 1986 Ford Taurus Sedan. The Taurus was Ford's new aerodynamic mid-size, but the most striking thing about it was its lack of grille. The Taurus owed more to its European counterparts than to the Tempo and bore practically no relation to the LTD it was replacing.

Above: The LeBaron Two-door Coupe was an attractive new model in 1987. It was completely different to the sedan and station wagon LeBaron, which used the K-car platform. The coupe's profile was described by some as 'Coke Bottle,' with its long hood and short little decklid. A three-speed automatic was standard on the sedan/wagon and optional on the coupe/convertible

Right: 1987 Dodge Daytona Shelby. The Daytona was Dodge's sporty little coupe. The Shelby Z was the top of the range model, with a 174hp Turbo engine. To enhance its appeal to the younger end of the buying market even further, a new Infinity Sound System and CD player was added to the options list.

Left: 1987 Oldsmobile Cutlass Ciera SL Coupe. The Cutlass Ciera continued to be Oldsmobile's best-selling nameplate in 1987. To celebrate, it introduced S and SL trim level coupes, as well as a Brougham station wagon. The Ciera's standard powertrain was a 2.5-liter Tech IV four-cylinder engine with an automatic transaxle.

Below: 1987 Oldsmobile Calais GT Coupe. Oldsmobile offered both a coupe and sedan version of the Calais GT. The GT's sporty image was enhanced by a rallye instrument cluster and leather wrapped sport steering wheel being provided as standard. The GT also offered Level III suspension.

Right: 1987 Oldsmobile Toronado Trofeo Coupe. The Oldsmobile Toronado had celebrated its 20th birthday the previous year with a major redesign, so it got a year off in 1987 and remained unchanged. It was the personal luxury car of the Olds range. The Trofeos were distinguished by a black valance with fog lamps, rocker panel extensions, and black wheel wells.

Below: 1987 Pontiac Grand Am. A more 'driver-oriented' approach was Pontiac's intention in introducing an SE derivative of the successful Grand Am range in 1986. For 1987, minor changes were made to trim and color ranges. The standard power plant was a 181cu in V6 fitted with multi-port fuel injection. The Grand Ams also gained a more aggressive body kit, rally tuned suspension, and a revised interior.

Above: 1987 Cadillac Coupe DeVille. Cadillac became increasingly security conscious throughout the 1980s, and chose 1987 to introduce a theft deterrent system using the underhood horn as an alarm. All major components were now also tagged with the car's individual vehicle identification number. The DeVille was also given a new grille.

Left: 1987 Buick Skyhawk Hatchback. 1987 was the year Buick gave its Skyhawk something to please the more sporty drivers. A turbocharged engine/manual transmission combination was introduced along with four new touring packages. By selecting a combination of these options, Skyhawk owners could more or less create themselves a bespoke vehicle.

Right: 1985 Ford Thunderbird. The Thunderbird remained relatively unchanged in 1985. Once again there were minor alterations to the grille and tail-lamps. This year also saw the introduction of a new Thunderbird emblem, which appeared on tail-lamp lenses, C pillars, and the upper grille header.

Below Right: 1986 Ford Mustang. The 1986 Mustang model line-up remained unchanged from the previous year — the LX two-door sedan or hatchback, the GT hatchback and convertible, and SVO. The SVO was still the 'ultimate Mustang,' with five-speed transmission and Hurst shifter that provided short quick throws as standard.

Bottom Right: 1986 Ford Thunderbird. The Thunderbird Fila was dropped from the line-up in 1986, reducing the range to three models. The Elan's interior became more luxurious, and the engines on all models were boosted in power output. The Thunderbird was now very similar to Mercury's Cougar.

Left: 1988 Ford Thunderbird. The Thunderbird changed little externally in 1988, although it did receive multi-point fuel injection to replace the earlier single-point system, which gave a welcome boost to its horsepower.

Below Left: 1988 Ford Mustang. In the wake of the 1987 redesign, Ford saw no need to bother with any major alterations to the Mustang in 1988. The only change, in fact, was a price increase. Sales continued to rise regardless, and as a consequence, plans were made to extend the Mustang's reign into the 1990s.

Bottom Left: 1989 Ford Mustang Ragtop.

Right: The Ford Mustang. started 1987 as a rear-drive hatchback model. The Mercury Capri was no more, which left the Mustang as Ford's only pony car. More disappearances followed — the SVO and the V6 engine. The LX and the GT were the two surviving models in the Mustang line up.

Below Right: 1987 Mercury Topaz. Mercury gave the Topaz new nitrogen-filled shock absorbers in 1987 and boosted its options list, with a new three speed automatic, and a part time four wheel drive system. A driver's airbag also became more widely available.

Left: 1987 Pontiac Sunbird Convertible. All Sunbird derivatives — coupe, hatchback, sedan, and convertible — could be ordered with a new GT specification for 1987. Convertibles were by far the most expensive of the Sunbird range, with sticker prices of $13,799 for the Sunbird SE and $15,569 for the Sunbird GT convertible, compared with $7,979 and $10,299 respectively for the Firebird sedan equivalents.

Below Left: 1987 Ford Taurus. The aero-styled Taurus was launched in mid-1986 so, understandably, little was done to alter it the following year as sales were going well. Mercury's Sables, which shared similar styling, were all V6-powered, while the Taurus still offered a 2.5-liter 4.

Right: 1987 Ford Tempo. Ford's Tempo was in its fourth season by 1987, and to mark this, it got a part time four-wheel drive option. By simply touching a switch on the dashboard, 4WD could be engaged, while the vehicle was moving. Power steering was now standard.

Below: 1988 Chrysler LeBaron. Chrysler's curvy LeBaron convertible came in two styles in 1988, the base (optimistically named the Highline) and Premium. Premium convertibles included a tilt steering wheel, cruise control, and power antenna. The LeBaron sedan and station wagon were built on a completely different platform to the other models and were more closely related to the Dodge Aries than to the coupes and convertibles.

Above: 1988 Buick Regal Ltd.
1988 was the year of the
new Regal for Buick. It now
had front-wheel drive along
with the most aerodynamic
design in Buick history.
Vertical ribs in the grille
meant the Regal could still be
identified as such. One of the
most interesting features of
the new design was its 'lubed
for life' suspension.

Left: 1988 Pontiac Grand Prix
SE. In 1988 a totally new
Pontiac Grand Prix range was
introduced. Three trim levels
were available — base Grand
Prix coupe, LE coupe, and SE
coupe, with sticker prices
ranging from $12,539 to
$15,249. Standard engine
was a 173cu in (2.8-liter) V6
producing 130hp.

1988 Buick Reatta. The newest addition to the Buick range was the 1988 Reatta. It had a sporty appearance and aerodynamic styling but still drove like a Buick. The Reatta was front-wheel drive, with independent suspension and fast ratio power steering.

Above: 1988 Oldsmobile Cutlass Supreme. During 1988 the Oldsmobile Cutlass Supreme range gained a new front-wheel drive platform. It was then offered in coupe form only, with three trim levels — base, SL, and International Series.

Right: 1988 Chevrolet S-10 Blazer. Little changed in appearance since its launch in 1982, the 1988 Chevrolet S-10 Blazer gained a new V6 engine option, a 4.3-liter unit producing 160hp. The base 2.5-liter engine produced only 98hp but the Blazer's part-time four-wheel drive system made up for lack of sheer power with off-road ability.

Left: 1988 Chrysler Voyager. The Voyager — and its Dodge equivalent, the Caravan — transformed the American auto industry by introducing the concept of the mini-van. Car-like comfort in a relatively compact package combined with enormous amounts of interior space for passengers and luggage proved irresistible to US families in particular. Soon all the other major auto manufacturers would follow Chrysler's example and launch their own vans.

Below: The 1988 Pontiac Bonneville SSE, introduced in 1988, was inspired by European auto design. It was a comfortable, spacious, and full-size sedan that also offered high performance and a high level of luxury touches in the cabin area, including a massive sound system.

Right: 1988 Buick Century. The Century line continued to offer coupe, sedan, and station wagon models into 1988. All Century models were given a new steering wheel but the main differences in this year were improvements to the 2.5 and 2.8-liter V6 engines.

Below: 1988 Cadillac Seville. Both the Seville and the Eldorado got a new front end in 1988. The Seville's suspension was refined to improve ride, and a touring suspension option was offered once again.

Above: 1988 Chevrolet Camaro. The performance model Z28 was dropped from the Camaro line-up in 1988. This resulted in the IROC-Z being promoted to a specific model rather than being just an option package. The number of convertibles produced this year rose from 1,000 the previous year to over 5,000.

Left: 1988 Pontiac Firebird Formula Sport Coupe. 1988 Pontiac Firebirds continued to be offered in Base, Formula, GTA, and Trans Am derivatives. The Formula package made available a 350cu in (5.7-liter) fuel-injected V8 in place of the standard 305cu in (5.0-liter) unit. The 5.7, also fitted to the GTA and Trans AM that year, produced 210hp.

Above: 1988 Chevrolet Cavalier Z24. The once lengthy Chevrolet Cavalier model range had been amputated to three in 1988: the base, RS, and Z24 models. It had, however, been given a more aerodynamic appearance with fresh sheet metal, a new grille and alterations to the headlamps. Although the RS convertible was dropped in this year, the Z24 ragtop remained.

Right: 1988 Chevrolet Beretta GT. 1988 was the first complete production year for Chevrolet's Corsica sedan and Beretta coupe. Consequently, few changes were made to either model.

Above: 1988 Buick Skyhawk Coupe. The Skyhawk line was extended to include a new S/E coupe by Buick in 1988. Improvements over the whole range were also made to ride, handling, durability, and easier maintenance and service — never a bad thing.

Left: 1988 Oldsmobile Delta 88. 1988 saw no major change to the Delta 88 line-up. It was the only one of General Motor's cars to offer an airbag in this year. Anti-lock brakes were also available. The Delta's standard powertrain was a rather impressive 3.8-liter sequential fuel-injected V6 coupled to a four-speed automatic transaxle.

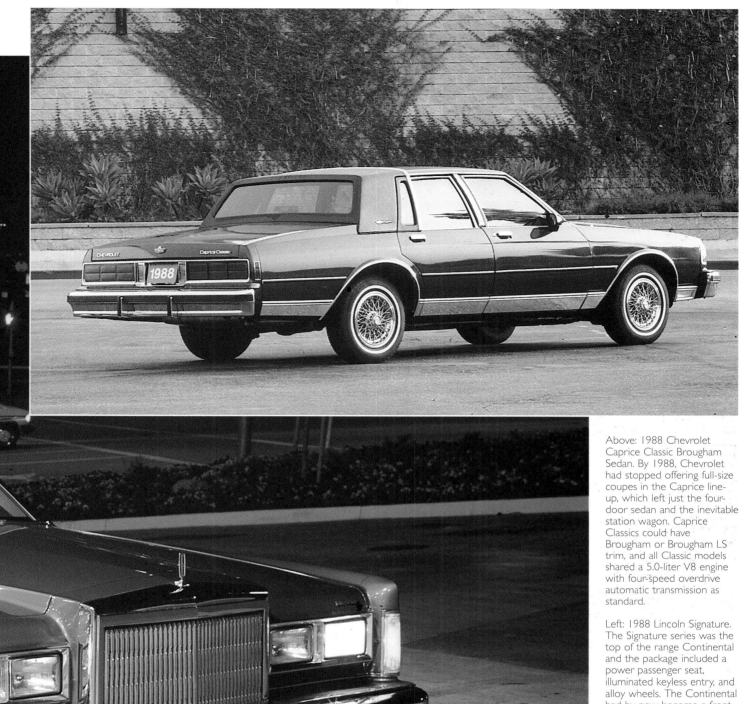

Above: 1988 Chevrolet Caprice Classic Brougham Sedan. By 1988, Chevrolet had stopped offering full-size coupes in the Caprice line-up, which left just the four-door sedan and the inevitable station wagon. Caprice Classics could have Brougham or Brougham LS trim, and all Classic models shared a 5.0-liter V8 engine with four-speed overdrive automatic transmission as standard.

Left: 1988 Lincoln Signature. The Signature series was the top of the range Continental and the package included a power passenger seat, illuminated keyless entry, and alloy wheels. The Continental had by now become a front-wheel drive sedan. It was the first FWD model from Lincoln, and also the first model with fewer than eight cylinders. It used the Thunderbird and Cougar's V6 instead.

Right: 1988 Chevrolet Celebrity Eurosport. The 1988 Eurosport option package on the Chevrolet Celebrity included special body trim as well as F41 sport suspension and a Getrag five-speed manual gearbox. It had bigger tires including the option of enormous P195/70R14 Goodyear Eagle GT+4 rubber.

Below: 1988 Chevrolet Corvette Convertible Coupe. The Corvette was available as both a convertible and a hatchback coupe in 1988. The biggest change to the Corvette's appearance in this year were its restyled six-slot wheels. Suspension modifications had also been made to provide better braking control by uprating its brake components.

Above: The bizarrely named 1988 Cadillac Fleetwood d'Elegance had all the electrical and mechanical refinements of the DeVille, plus a standard items list that ranged from cruise control to an illuminated vanity mirror. Six new exterior colors were offered for 1988.

Left: 1988 Oldsmobile Cutlass Supreme Classic Coupe. Oldsmobile's old timer, the Cutlass Supreme Classic was phased out half way through 1988. The old G-bodied rear-drive favorite was replaced by the brand new GM10 front drive Cutlass Supreme. This came in coupe form only.

Right: 1988 Ford LTD Crown. The two-door coupe dropped out of the LTD Crown Victoria line-up in 1988. The remaining full-size Ford sedans got a front and rear restyle and they also got wraparound taillamps. This was the first restyle the LTD had had in almost ten years. Both base and LX models were fitted with 150hp 5.0-liter V8 engine.

Below: 1988 Ford Escort GT Coupe. Although the Escort began 1988 looking the same as ever, it was replaced half way through by a modified second series. It got new fenders, taillamps, and body side moldings. The Escort was now no longer Ford's best seller — the Taurus had stolen that title.

Left: 1989 Pontiac Grand Prix LE Sedan. The Pontiac Grand Prix continued to attract attention in 1989 thanks to its combination of sharp styling, reasonable performance, and sporty interior. Total production during the year was a creditable 136,750 units.

Below: 1988 Buick Century Ltd. 1989 saw Buick produce an updated Century. It changed its front and rear appearance, altering the positioning of the lamps. The Limited sedan was now fitted with the UJ5 instrument panel gauge option as standard equipment. The Limited coupe model was cancelled in this year.

Above: 1988 Chevrolet Camaro RS Sport Coupe. The RS was the cheaper of the two Camaro versions that Chevrolet offered the public in 1989. The RS and the IROC-Z were available as hatchbacks or convertibles and both had been fitted with a new anti-theft mechanism — due to its popularity with non-paying consumers of Camaros. The RS had a deliberately small engine, to keep the cost of insuring it to a minimum.

Right: 1988 Chevrolet Corsica Four-door Sedan. Chevrolet added a four-door hatchback sedan to the Corsica four-door notchback version in 1989.

Above: 1988 Oldsmobile Cutlass Supreme International Coupe Series. 1989 was the first full production year for the Cutlass Supreme. No major changes had taken place over this period, but there had been minor refinements. The International series had more standard features than ever, including power mirrors, fog lamps, and remote lock control.

Left: 1988 Oldsmobile Cutlass Supreme Coupe. The Cutlass Supreme was offered in coupe version only in base, SL, and International series trim. Mid-model-year, a 3.1-liter V6 engine appeared in conjunction with a four-speed automatic transaxle. This replaced the existing 2.8-liter V6.

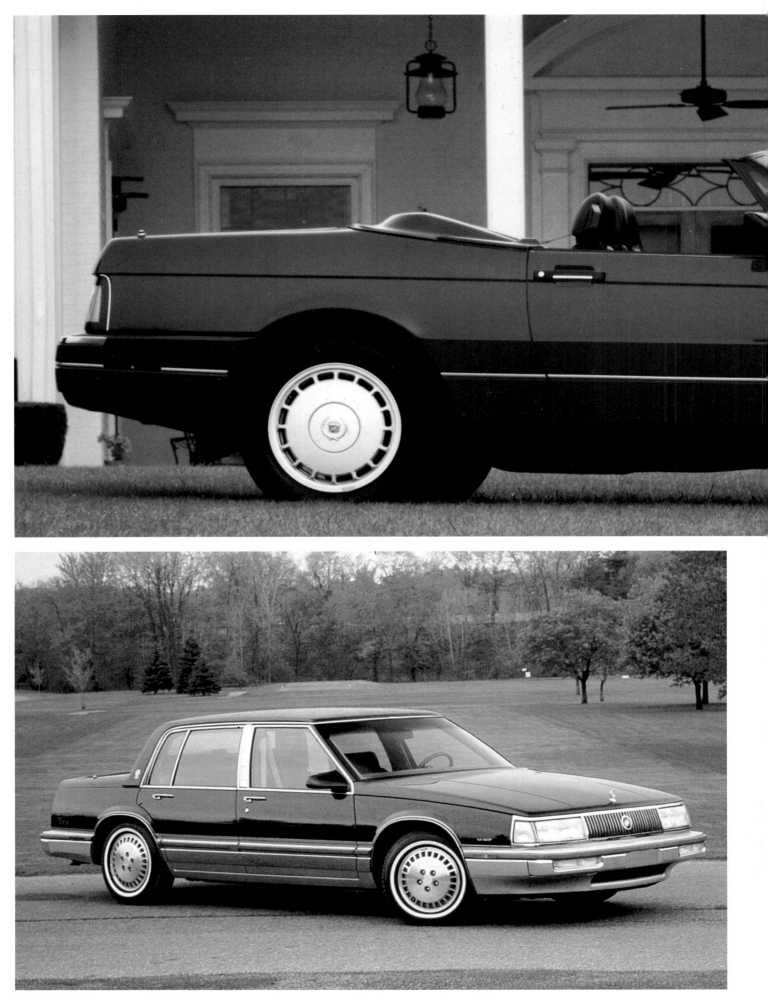

Left: 1989 Cadillac Allante. Cadillac gave the Allante more power in 1989, with a performance improving 4.5-liter fuel injection engine. This gave an impressive 17% increase to its horsepower and knocked 0.8 seconds off its zero-60 acceleration time. It gained speed-dependent suspension for a greater variety of ride/handling characteristics.

Below Left: 1989 Mercury Cougar. The Cougar was Mercury's show stealer in 1989, appearing for the first time in completely new form. Again, it was closely related to the Thunderbird. It weighed 400lb more than the previous incarnation, despite being smaller. Its wheelbase had grown and it now had four wheel independent suspension. The XR7 remained the sports model.

Far Left: 1989 Buick Park Avenue Ultra Sedan. This was the most noticeable development in Buick's 1989 Electra range. It was billed as the 'ultimate in Buick luxury,' a serious bid to compete in the luxury sedan market. Sterling silver lower accent paint treatment and silver accent body stripe distinguished the Ultra from the standard Park Avenue.

The 1990s

The start of the 1990s was neither a happy nor a productive time for the US auto makers. The total market, ravaged by recession, hardly exceeded 9.25 million units in 1990, then fell back to a dismal 8.1 million in 1991, steadied at 8.2 million the following year, and crept up to 8.4 million by 1993. Since then, the market for cars has not improved greatly — the total figure was still only 8.5 million for 1996 — but cars represent only one part of the complete US auto market.

Add light trucks to the equation and the total market reached just over 15 million units — the best year since 1985. Trucks — defined as vehicles under 14,000lb gross vehicle weight — have now reached close to 45% of the total US market. Modern US men and women have demonstrated very clearly that pick-up trucks, utility vehicles (SEVs), and recreational vehicles (RVs) are the vehicles they want to buy in the late 1990s.

Their popularity is due to a number

326

Above: 1990 Ford Festiva. Needing to fulfill a market desire for a sub-compact car, and having nothing of its own to offer, Ford looked to Mazda of Japan for an answer. Mazda, in turn, looked to one of its Korean subsidiaries to manufacture the 1.3-liter Festiva, a model broadly similar to the Mazda 121 sold in Japan and Europe.

Left: 1990 Ford Thunderbird. Having been so dramatically redesigned in 1989, the Thunderbird changed little in 1990. The base and LX models retained their automatic engines, while the Super Coupe had a five-speed manual gearbox as standard.

of factors. They satisfy both the social and the commercial needs of the modern consumer. In addition, rising incomes in a growing US economy and stable fuel prices mean that large vehicles remain affordable. Manufacturers have also embraced the pick-up/SEV ethos with enthusiasm, not least because, since the vehicles tend to be based on similar — in some cases identical — platforms, so the vehicles lend themselves to a high degree of manufacturing flexibility between different body styles.

Whether the light truck segment can continue expanding long term remains to be seen, not least because the US government and states such as California continue to pressure auto manufacturers to reduce fuel consumption and exhaust emissions — something that is hard to do with large, heavy vehicles powered by powerful, large capacity engines.

Though the Japanese importers continued to thrive during the early part of the decade, no longer could the blame

Above: 1990 Ford Mustang Convertible. This continued to be a popular choice for Mustang buyers. A special limited edition convertible in white and emerald green was rumored to be on the horizon in 1990, but finally proved too expensive to produce and never appeared.

Left: Chrysler Voyager Town & Country. For 1990, the Town & Country gained a modified interior and, more importantly, a new 3.3-liter V6 version which went on sale alongside the existing 2.5-liter Voyager and replaced the older 3.0-liter derivative. A four-wheel drive system developed by Steyr in Austria was also available at extra cost.

Below: 1990 Buick Estate Wagon. This was the station wagon of the former LeSabre range, with a V8 5.0-litre engine, five doors, and enormous interior space, with eight-person seating capacity.

be placed at their door for the poor performance of the domestic manufacturers. Quite simply, in a shrunken market, everyone involved in the auto industry was forced to make some hard and painful decisions, almost all of which involved retrenchment, plant closures, and layoffs.

Chrysler was again in financial difficulties at the start of the decade. And Oldsmobile was more than once threatened with extinction. In the event, both survived but a number of importers — Sterling (Rover) of the UK, Daihatsu of Japan, Peugeot of France, and Yugo from Yugoslavia, all pulled out of the US.

Since all were selling in extremely small volumes, these withdrawals did little to solve the massive overcapacity problems that the US was facing. GM, Ford, and Chrysler all embarked on massive cost-cutting programmes.

The one bright light on the horizon was GM's Saturn project. This was a new line aimed at competing head-on with the Japanese and matching or even exceeding their quality and their efficiency levels. Everything about the pro-

gramme was innovative, with virtually nothing carried over from existing GM products or practices.

GM hoped that, by developing a new car with new engines, new transmissions, new production plant, new deal with unions at that plant, and even new franchise agreements with the dealers aiming to sell the cars, they would be able to start a revolution within GM. Saturn was important in itself as a means of beating the Japanese at their own game. But it was also crucial in that it would represent a sort of beacon, showing the rest of the massive GM organization the way forward in a global auto industry that the US makers would never again be able to dominate as they had in the past.

Saturn cars went on sale in late 1990 though initially it was disappointing how few cars found their way to willing customers due to production problems at the plant.

It was also disappointing that for a brand based on the bedrock of better build quality and design integrity than ever before, Saturn should suffer two

Left: 1990 Cadillac Brougham. A well-respected luxury car, the Brougham was the only Cadillac range to have front-wheel drive at the start of the 1990s. The Brougham was restyled in 1989 and its power and performance were boosted in 1990 thanks to the adoption of a new 5.7-liter V8 power unit.

Below: 1990 Chevrolet Geo Tracker. An all-terrain vehicle, the Chevrolet Tracker has two- or four-wheel drive, transfer box and a 1.6-liter 97hp engine. Designed, engineered, and built by Suzuki in Japan, and launched in the USA in 1988, the Geo Tracker was sold in Japan and Europe as the Suzuki Vitara.

Below: 1990 Chevrolet Corsica Beretta. Originally launched at the beginning of 1987, the Corsica sedan and Beretta coupe originally had 2.3-liter 16V engines. Later, in 1994, the rather gutless old 2.3 was replaced by a more powerful 2.2-liter 122hp engine.

major recalls. In 1991, some 1,800 cars had to be recalled and the owners were given new cars. If that exercise was not costly enough, in 1993 a second recall was necessary. Every car built between 1990 and 1993 had to be adapted to prevent potential engine fires.

The cost to GM of these recalls was immense but the experience does not seem to have put off American car buyers. After its slow start in 1990, Saturn sales rose to 75,000 in 1991 and then took off to reach just under 200,000 in 1992 and 225,000 the following year.

GM also attacked the more compact Japanese imports from another direction during the early 1990s, launching the Geo range under its Chevrolet banner. By this time, GM had decided that the maxim 'if you can't beat them, join them' made increasing sense, because the Chevy Geo was no more than a US name for yet more Japanese imports, cars built for GM by arch-rival Toyota back in Japan.

But if GM has had to eat some humble pie in adopting the Geo range, it cannot be said to have been a poor

decision. Though sales started off rather slowly, very soon the small and economical Geos started appealing to a younger car-buying public and total sales to date can be counted in their millions.

Ford started the decade with a major cost-cutting exercise and followed this up with some innovative pricing policies, designed to make the whole process of choosing and buying a new car far simpler and less stressful for the customer. Ford started with its Escort range during 1991 when it threw away its existing price lists and declared that all Escort LX cars fitted with a manual transmission would cost the same, whether a sedan, hatchback, or wagon was chosen. Automatic versions cost a little more, but the principal remained in that the price of any body variant was constant.

Encouraged by the success of the Escort program, a similar pricing strategy was rolled out over the Ford Thunderbird and Mercury Cougar ranges for 1993.

But it was not just by clever pricing policies that Ford has weathered the difficulties of the 1990s better than most. It

Left: 1990 Pontiac Grand Prix LE Sedan. Pontiac's Grand Prix range had been first launched in the late 1980s. By 1990 the range was improved by the addition of a sedan version and by the adoption of new engines. Quickest was a 213hp 3.4-liter V6, followed by a 2.3-liter 16V unit producing 162hp, and finally a 141hp 2.3-liter V6.

Below: 1990 Pontiac Trans Sport. Of all the MPVs available at the start of the 1990s, the most stylish and elegant was Pontiac's Trans Sport. Originally introduced in late 1989, the Trans Sport was powered by a 3.1-liter V6 mounted transversally and driving the front wheels via a standard automatic transmission.

Above: 1990 Pontiac Firebird Trans Am GTA. The Trans Am GTA stood at the pinnacle of Pontiac's Firebird range of performance sports cars. With 243hp available from its 5.7-liter V8, the GTA was good for a top speed of over 140mph by the time the rev limiter cut in, and took only 6.5 seconds to accelerate from 0-60mph.

also succeeded in bringing the right products to the marketplace at the right time.

Chrysler too got out of trouble by cutting costs and by launching new products that consumers wanted to buy. Having started the decade deeply in the red, Chrysler looked long and hard at the Japanese way of building close relationships with suppliers in order to boost quality levels and reduce manufacturing costs. The first concrete example of Chrysler's new found preoccupation with building cars specifically according to customer desires came with the Neon in 1994.

The neatly styled sub-compact car came as standard with a full and generous specification, a sophisticated multi-valve engine and — most important of all — a sticker price some thousands of dollars below its Japanese competitors.

The other US auto makers also took on board the lesson they had learned from the Japanese — that quality was critically important because modern consumers would no longer put up with poorly built and unreliable autos. GM's Saturn and Ford's Taurus — two other 1990s' introductions were further examples of how much progress the American auto manufacturers were making — both started scoring well in the all-important J.D. Power industry quality ratings.

Those ratings had been launched in the 1980s at which time the average US car had eight faults and the Japanese makers invariably took the top ten places. By 1990 any car scoring one fault or less would certainly make it into the top ten. But by 1993, no less than 48 US cars had achieved that mark, or less than one fault per car.

Quality had become of age, and the US auto industry became all the stronger because of it.

Above: 1990 Cadillac Seville STS. The Seville Touring Sedan, with its luxurious interior, effortless performance from a 4.9-liter V8, and smooth ride thanks to an all-independent suspension system, offered the grace and pace of a typical Cadillac even if the space was limited in the STS's more compact bodywork.

Left: 1990 Cadillac Eldorado Touring Coupe. The Eldorado had been downsized in 1986, when its new E-body — on the same platform as the Seville — was introduced. It lost 16in in length but gained interior space thanks to front-wheel drive. This gave the Eldorado a sporty yet elegant look, and to back this up it was fitted with a purposeful transverse mounted 4.5-liter V8 engine.

Above: 1990 Chevrolet Beretta Convertible. The big news for the Beretta range in 1990 was the launch of a new convertible model. The standard Beretta power unit was a four-cylinder 2.2-liter producing 96hp, but Beretta GTZ versions were fitted with a considerably more pugnacious 182hp 2.3-liter 16V engine.

Right: 1990 Cadillac Sedan DeVille. A lengthy, luxury car, the DeVille and the similar Fleetwood Sixty Special were originally launched in 1984. With front-wheel drive and a Cadillac's 4.5-liter V8 injection engine, the DeVille had a maximum speed of around 125mph. In 1991, the 4.5-liter engine was replaced by a new and more powerful 4.9-liter V8.

336

Left: 1991 Ford Thunderbird. New for 1991 was a flagship Ford Thunderbird version, fitted with a 4.9-litre V8 pushing out 203hp. This was not as powerful as the supercharged 3.8-litre V6 which produced 213hp and gave a top speed of over 136mph, but the V8 was quieter and more refined while still being good for around 125mph.

Below: 1991 Chevrolet Caprice. Launched in 1990, the Caprice was *the* big Chevrolet, with its aerodynamic body and 4.3-litre V8 engine. The Caprice Classic Wagon appeared in 1991, followed by the Impala SS saloon in 1993. Later, in 1994 new 4.3- and 5.7-litre engines were brought out.

Above: 1991 Dodge Stealth R/T. Practically identical to the Mitsubishi 3000 GT on which it was based, the sporty Dodge Stealth was called the Intrepid when it appeared as a concept car in 1988. It was launched as the Stealth in 1990. The R/T was fitted with a twin-turbo 3.0-liter V6 producing 305hp. Top speed was over 155mph and 0-60mph acceleration was a rubber burning sub-six seconds.

Right: 1991 Chevrolet Blazer. Available in both rear-wheel and all-wheel drive versions, the Chevy Blazer S-10 was originally fitted with a rather feeble 2.5-liter four-cylinder or 2.8-liter V6. By the early 1990s, however, it was only sold with a more powerful 162hp 4.3-liter V6.

Left: 1991 Oldsmobile Cutlass Ciera SL. While lesser Cutlass Ciera models had to make do with a 2.5-liter four-cylinder engine, the more expensive SL versions benefited from the more powerful and infinitely smoother 3.3-liter V6. A Cruiser SL station wagon was also available.

Below: 1991 Oldsmobile Bravada. Based on Chevy's S-10 Blazer and GMC's S-15 Jimmy, the Bravada offered a high level of specification such as standard air-conditioning, anti-lock brakes, alloy wheels, and cruise control. Power came from a 4.3-liter V6.

Above: 1991 Oldsmobile
Trofeo. A spin-off from
the Toronado, the Trofeo
featured four headlamps
and trim changes such as
body-colored from air dam.
Power came from a 3.8-liter
V6 matched to a four-speed
automatic transmission.

Right: 1991 Oldsmobile
Regency Elite. The 1991
Oldsmobile 98 was available
either as a Regency Elite
Sedan or Touring Sedan.
Restyled with bodywork
some 9.5in longer than
before, the Regency Elite
sported a 3.8-liter V6 mated
to a new Turbo-Hydra-matic
transmission.

Above: 1991 Oldsmobile Custom Cruiser. Still retaining Oldsmobile's tried and tested 5.0-liter V8, the Custom Cruiser also kept rear-wheel drive from the good old days. But this mature technology was hidden by a sleek new body featuring flush glass and a vista roof.

Left: Buick Park Avenue. Launched at the start of the 1990s, the Park Avenue and Park Avenue Ultra models featured smooth and sleek new bodywork, and a 173hp 3.8-liter V8 engine. Inside, luxury, space, and comfort were the watchwords.

Above: 1991 Oldsmobile Silhouette. In essence a rebadged Pontiac Trans Sport, the Silhouette was improved for 1991 with standard rear heating, air conditioning, and added interior specification. The standard power option remained the 3.1-liter V6 powering the front wheels via a three-speed automatic transmission.

Right: 1991 Dodge Daytona. The transverse engine, front-wheel drive Daytona was available with 2.5-liter, 2.5-liter turbo, and 3.0-liter V6 engine options. It looked sporty with its fastback design but there was little particularly impressive about its performance.

Below: 1991 Ford Mustang. 1991 saw little change to the appearance of the evergreen Ford Mustang, which was still available with a fairly pedestrian 2.3-liter four-cylinder engine in LX versions or, alternatively, a more performance orientated 4.9-liter V8 in the Mustang GT and GT Convertible derivatives.

Overleaf: 1991 Mercury Capri. The elegant compact 2+2 Mercury Capri had a Ghia-designed body and an interior by ItalDesign. But the truth is that all this Italian design input was little more than a smokescreen aimed at hiding the fact that underneath was a Japanese Mazda 323 platform, 1.6-liter engine, and five-speed manual or three-speed auto transmission.

Above: 1992 Ford Thunderbird. For 1992, the LX versions were fitted with a 142hp V6 while the Thunderbird Super Coupe was available fitted with with a 213hp supercharged V6 or the 203hp V8 first introduced the year before.

Right: 1992 Ford Mustang. No major changes were made to the Mustang range for 1992. As before, it was available in two- and three-door coupe form, or as a two-door convertible. Engines were either a 2.3-liter four-cylinder producing 106hp or else a lusty 228hp 4.9-liter V8.

Left: 1992 Buick LeSabre. The four-door LeSabre was launched in 1992 fitted with a 172hp 3.8-liter V6 mated to a four-speed GM Hydra-Matic automatic transmission. A large and imposing sedan, it seated six in comfort.

Below: 1992 Ford Bronco. Improved in 1992, the Bronco incorporated a higher specification inside and some minor body revisions. Four- and five-speed manual, and a Cruise-O-Matic auto transmission were available mated either to a 147hp 4.9-liter six-cylinder or 188hp 4.9-liter V8 engine.

Above: 1992 Buick Roadmaster. With a name first used as long ago as 1936, the range was relaunched in autumn 1990, based on the Chevrolet Caprice 1991. Available as both a sedan and a station wagon, the new Roadmaster was powered by a 264hp 5.7-liter V8.

Right: 1992 Cadillac Seville. Having been unveiled as a prototype in Detroit in January 1991, the new Seville reached the showrooms in the Fall of 1992. At that time the Seville was powered by Cadillac's 4.6-liter 32-valve Northstar STS V8 engine.

Above: 1992 Cadillac Coupe DeVille. The DeVille shared the Eldorado's 4.9-liter V8 came as either a two-door coupe or four-door sedan. Fleetwood versions were also available in coupe and sedan versions, though the Fleetwood 60 Special and the Touring were only produced as four-door sedans.

Left: 1992 Cadillac Eldorado. The Eldorado was freshened in 1991 with a redesigned new and sleek body. Under the hood was a 4.9-liter 305hp V8 that provided both grace and pace for Cadillac's flagship coupe.

Right: The Fleetwood 60 Special Cadillac DeVille was one of the largest luxury cars on the US market in the early 1990s. Originally launched in 1984 with front-wheel drive, in 1991, the original 4.5-liter V8 engine was replaced by a new 4.9-liter V8.

Below: 1992 Cadillac Allante. Available as a hardtop cabriolet or coupe, the Allante had the mechanics of a Cadillac mated to body-work and interior styled by Pininfarina in Italy. It was launched in 1986 and in 1989 a 4.5-liter V8 version appeared. In January 1992, power was improved thanks to the adoption of a 4.6-liter 32-valve V8.

Above: 1992 Chevrolet Blazer K Yukon. Launched in 1992, the Chevrolet Tahoe-GMC Yukon is a large four-wheel drive all-terrain vehicle fitted with a rugged 5.7-liter V8 258hp engine. In 1994, a 6.5-liter V8 turbodiesel engine became available, and in 1995 a five-door version was added to the range.

Left: 1992 Chevrolet Cavalier RS convertible. New engines had been adopted for the Chevrolet Cavalier range in 1990, offering 112hp (2.2-liter four-cylinder) or 142hp (3.1-liter V6) respectively. First revealed at the Detroit Auto Show in January 1991 was a new convertible version.

Right: The export version of the Dodge Viper was the Chrysler Viper RT/10. An uncompromising supersports car, its prototype was shown at the Detroit Auto Show in January 1989 and received such a rapturous response that a production model appeared in 1992. The Viper has an 8.0-liter V10 406hp engine and a six-speed gearbox.

Below: 1992 Chevrolet Blazer S-10. For 1992, power output of the mighty S-10 was boosted to 162hp and 203hp for the two normally aspirated 4.3-liter V6 engines on offer.

Above: 1992 Pontiac Bonneville SE. Celebrating its 35th year in 1992, the Pontiac Bonneville was restyled and gained higher levels of standard specification that year. The regular Bonneville engine was a 3.8-liter six-cylinder unit fitted with an Eaton Rootes-type supercharger to boost power output to 205hp.

Left: 1992 Dodge Spirit ES. The Spirit, a four-door saloon derived from the A-Cars, replaced the Dodge Aries model. Launched in 1988, a sports model appeared in 1991 fitted with a more powerful 2.2-liter DACT 16-valve 227hp engine.

Right: 1992 Chrysler New Yorker Salon. A style-free, though luxurious sedan, the New Yorker was powered by Chrysler's familiar 3.3-liter V6. Its plush interior could be ordered with tufted leather complemented by an optional landau vinyl roof.

Below: 1992 Chevrolet Typhoon. Flagship of the Blazer S-10/GMC Jimmy range, the Typhoon is fitted with a turbocharged 284hp version of GM's 4.3-liter V6.

Above: 1992 Pontiac SSEi. Top dog of the Bonneville line-up, the SSEi incorporated a range of high-tech novelties such as heated front windscreen, a head-up instrument display, remote keyless entry, and an eight-speaker sound system. It also was fitted with a more powerful supercharged version of the 3.8-litre V6.

Left: The 1992 Chrysler Le Baron Coupe GTC was powered by a 3.0-litre V6 producing 141hp, and the same engine was fitted to the GTC convertible. Lesser Le Barons had to make do with a 100hp 2.5-liter four-cylinder unit.

Above: 1992 Pontiac Firebird. By 1992 the full Firebird line-up included Firebird, Firebird Formula, Trans Am, and Trans Am GTA versions. A convertible had been launched in 1991 — the first Firebird convertible since 1970. The base Firebird was powered by Pontiac's 3.1-liter V6.

Right: 1992 GMC Suburban. When size is what matters most, the Suburban truck comes into its own, offering enormous interior space for passengers and their luggage.

Above: 1992 Chevrolet Camaro RS Coupe. Celebrating its 25th anniversary in 1992, the Camaro RS Coupe offered a choice of 3.1-liter V6 or 5.0-liter V8 engines. An even more powerful 5.7-liter engine was offered on the flagship Camaro Z28.

Left: 1992 Pontiac Trans Am. Powered by a 5.0-liter V8 and fitted with what was described as 'Rally-Tuned' sports suspension, the Pontiac Trans Am was available in both coupe and convertible versions. With total Firebird production topping the 25,000 mark during 1992, the two-seat sports model showed no sign of losing its popularity.

Right: 1992 Chevrolet Corvette LT-1. Power from the V8 was upped to 304hp in 1992, offering a potential top speed of over 155mph and 0-60mph acceleration in 4.9 seconds.

Below: The 1992 Chevrolet Corvette ZR-1 was even quicker, with a 174mph max, and 0-60mph acceleration in a shattering 4.3 seconds.

Above: 1992 Pontiac Grand Am SE. Pontiac's compact front-wheel drive Grand Am model was available in both two-door coupe and four-door sedan versions. Power outputs ranged from 122hp right up to 182hp for the sophisticated 2.3-liter DOHC 16V engine that was introduced in late 1991.

Left: 1992 Chevrolet Corsica LT Sedan. Sharing platform and mechanicals with the Beretta coupe, the Corsica sedan was fitted as standard with a 2.2-liter 112hp four-cylinder engine but a more powerful 142hp V6 was also available.

Right: Ford Mustang. For 1993, an even more powerful Mustang model made its appearance — the Mustang Cobra fitted with a 238hp version of Ford's 4.9-litre V8. The extra 10hp gave the Cobra a top speed of over 143mph and acceleration from 0-60mph in just 5.9 seconds.

Left: 1993 Ford Bronco II. With its 5.3-litre V8, the Ford Bronco II was short on neither power nor size. Its presence — whether on or off the road — was immense.

Below Left: 1993 Buick Skylark. The Skylark had earned a reputation for being both sporty and luxurious, ever since first launched in 1980. That launch had represented a watershed for Buick, introducing front-wheel drive and all-coil suspension. During the 1990s new versions of the Skylark were introduced that served to maintain Buick's reputation.

Above: 1993 Buick Century. 1993 saw new engines being introduced to the Century. The range started with a 2.2-liter four-cylinder unit producing 122hp, though a 3.1-liter V6 producing a healthier 162hp was still available. Both sedan and eight-seat wagon versions of the Century were in the showrooms.

Right: 1993 Cadillac Fleetwood. By now Cadillac's sole remaining rear-wheel drive model, the Fleetwood and Fleetwood Brougham gained new 5.7-liter V8s in 1992, sufficient to provide stately performance to a maximum of around 124mph with 0-60mph acceleration in just over 10 seconds.

Left: 1993 Buick Regal Gran Sport Coupe. Styling and trim details were changed for 1993 on the Buick Regal range. Though the standard V6 was a 3.1-liter unit producing 142hp, the Gran Sport versions were fitted with a 3.8-liter V6 good for 172hp.

Below: 1993 GMC Astro 4WD. Ready to go anywhere, carrying just about anything . . . the massive GMC Astro was available with a four-wheel drive option for those needing to get off the beaten track while still transporting a family and most of its belongings.

Right: 1993 Chevrolet Corvette Coupe. Having gained a power boost in 1992, with even base models now pushing out 304hp from their 5.7-liter V8s, the Corvette remained one of the American motor industry's strongest icons. Both the coupe with its targa roof and the alternative full convertible models were equally popular.

Below: 1993 Ford Thunderbird. 1993 saw few major changes to the Thunderbird. Power output of the base 3.8-liter V6 model remained at 142hp, while the Thunderbird Super Coupe was available with either a 3.8-liter V6 super-charged engine producing 213hp, or else the 203hp 4.9-liter V8.

Left: 1994 Chrysler Voyager. Chrysler's minivans continued to dominate the market during the early 1990s, with the Dodge Caravan and the Plymouth Voyager being the USA's top sellers by a clear margin.

Below: 1994 Eagle Vision. The Concord was Chrysler's upmarket version of the company's latest 'LH' mid-sized sedan. Other derivatives were the Dodge Intrepid and the Eagle Vision. The cars were powered either by a 3.3-liter V6 producing 153hp, or by a 3.5-liter 24-valve V6 that boosted the output to a more healthy 214hp.

Above: 1994 Ford Mustang. New engines gave the Mustang a new lease of life in late 1993. Base models gained a 147hp 3.8-litre V6 while performance GT models were fitted with a 4.9-litre V8 producing up to 243hp.

Left: 1994 Ford Aspire. Ford's sub-compact Aspire was a 1.3-litre hatchback which replaced the Festiva during 1993. The Aspire was a Mazda design, sold as the Mazda 121 in other markets, and also as the Kia Pride in Korea, where the Aspire was manufactured.

Right: 1995 Chrysler Neon. Saloon or coupe, the Neon was launched in 1993, replacing the Dodge Shadow and Plymouth Sundance. The Neon was designed specifically to beat the Japanese at their own game by offering a high quality subcompact model, highly specified, and at a highly competitive price. The Neon was originally launched with a 2.0-liter 147hp engine under the hood, and in 1998, a 1.8-liter 116hp version was introduced.

Below: 1995 Chevrolet Blazer. A new version of the evergreen Blazer was launched at the Detroit Auto Show at the beginning of 1994. Three- and five-door models were available, both powered by a 4.3-liter 198hp V6, and driving all four wheels via a center differential and either a five-speed manual or automatic transmission.

Above: 1995 Pontiac Firebird Cabrio. By now Pontiac's only rear-wheel drive offering, the Firebird soldiered on in both coupe and convertible versions. Built in Canada, the muscle cars gained traction control and new color options during 1995.

Left: 1995 Chrysler New Yorker. Though based on the LH sedans, the New Yorker was some five inches longer, to provide even more interior and trunk space. Only one engine was offered — a 3.5-liter V6 producing 214hp.

Top: 1995 Buick Regal Coupe. Biggest news concerning the 1995 Buick Regal range was a new interior. Two- and four-door versions remained on offer, with all Regals fitted with V6 engines of either 3.1- or 3.6-liter capacity.

Above: 1995 Pontiac Grand Am Sedan. Pontiac's 150hp 2.3-liter DOHC Quad 4 engine became standard for the Grand Am in 1995. As before, both two-door coupe and four-door sedan versions were available. For those requiring rather more performance, the Grand Am GT — also available as coupe or sedan — had a 155hp 3.1-liter V6 under the hood.

Right: 1995 Cadillac Seville STS. Minor body modifications and a more powerful engine were given to the Seville STS for 1995. The power was upped to 305hp from its 4.6-liter 32-valve V8, providing genuine 150mph performance to go alongside the Cadillac's undoubted style and prestige.

Above: 1996 Chrysler New Yorker. In terms of exterior appearance there is little to differentiate the New Yorker from the LHS. The New Yorker, however, was loaded with every conceivable extra including traction control and leather seat trim.

Right: 1996 Chrysler LHS Though based on the Concorde, the Chrysler LHS is six inches longer and provides more passenger space and trunk area. Only one engine was offered at launch — the 214hp 3.5-liter V6.

Left: 1996 Dodge Avenger. Launched late in 1995, the Avenger replaced the Daytona which had been around for so long. Though styled by Chrysler people, the Avenger is built by Mitsubishi at their Illinois plant on a lightly modified Mitsubishi Galant platform. Engines are Dodge's own 2.0-liter four-cylinder unit or Mitsubishi's 2.5-liter V6.

Below: 1996 Dodge Ram Club Cab 1500 4x4. The beefy Ram pick-up range was extended to include a Club Cab version from the 1995 model year. Various engines were available and alongside the standard two-wheel drive models was this 4x4.

Above: 1996 Dodge Stratus. Replacing the Spirit sedan, the Stratus was yet another example of Chrysler's 'cab-forward' design. Like the very similar Chrysler Cirrus, the Dodge Stratus was offered with 2.0-liter 132hp, 2.4-liter 140hp and 2.5-liter V6 164hp engine options.

Right: 1996 Eagle Summit Sedan. Equipped with 1.5- and 1.8-liter engines, the Eagle Summit range, which was based upon the Japanese Mitsubishi Mirage design, was renewed in 1994.

Left: 1996 Dodge Stealth. Practically identical to the Japanese Mitsubishi 3000 GT, the sporty Stealth gained more power in 1994 when the output of its most powerful engine derivative was increased from 304hp to 324hp.

Below: 1996 Eagle Summit Wagon. The complete Eagle Summit range consisted of three-door hatchback, four-door sedan, and five-door station wagon versions, each based upon an equivalent Mitsubishi Mirage model.

Right: 1996 Eagle Vision. A modern sedan belonging to the LH generation, the Eagle Vision was launched as a prototype in Detroit in January 1992, and went into production in Canada in the following summer. It was fitted with a V6 engine, available in two versions, with two or four valves per cylinder, and producing 163hp or 213hp respectively.

Below: 1996 Eagle Talon. Built by Diamond-Star USA, Chrysler's joint venture with Mitsubishi of Japan, the Eagle Talon was a sporty little coupe with front-wheel drive, also sold as the Mitsubishi Eclipse. A new version appeared in 1994, with 2.0-liter 141hp and 2.0-liter supercharged 213hp engines.

Above: 1996 Plymouth Voyager. A parallel model to the Dodge Caravan, the monospace Plymouth Voyager had started America's love affair with the minivan when first launched in Autumn 1983. The very latest derivative, featuring a more rounded body design, was launched in January 1995. It offered three engine sizes, ranging from 2.4-liter 16-valve to 3.3-liter V6.

Left: 1996 Plymouth Breeze. Successor to the Acclaim, the Breeze was launched in January 1995 at both the Detroit and Los Angeles motor shows and went on sale shortly after. A sedan was available with either 2.0-liter 16-valve or 2.4-liter 16-valve engine options.

Above: 1996 Dodge Viper GTS. Powerful and beautiful in equal measure, the Dodge Viper GTS is the hardtop spin-off of the RT/10 roadster, fitted with the same 8.0-liter V10 and six-speed gear box and boasting a maximum speed of 185mph. Launched as a prototype in Detroit in 1993, the GTS was produced as a series model in 1996.

Left: 1996 Buick Electra/Park Avenue. In 1996 the Buick Park Avenue range was relaunched with modern and sleek new bodywork. Two versions were available, both powered by a 3.8-liter V6, but producing 208hp and 243hp respectively.

Far Left, Bottom: The Buick Regal was available with two different engines in the mid-1990s. A 162hp 3.1-liter V6 provided a maximum speed of some 118mph, while the 172hp 3.8-liter V6 was good for 121mph.

Below: 1996 Pontiac Trans Am. For 1996, 3.4-litre engines were dropped from the Pontiac Firebird/Trans Am range, leaving just the 203hp 3.8-litre V6 and the mighty 288hp 5.7-litre V8. The latter was still sufficient to propel the Trans Am to at some 155mph with sub-six-second 0-60mph acceleration to match.

Right: 1997 Dodge Durango. Successor to the Ramcharger, the new Dodge Durango is a four-wheel drive vehicle offering three different engine options. Base models have a 177hp 3.9-liter V6, but drivers seeking more power can opt for either 237hp 5.2-liter V8 or 250hp 5.9-liter V8 engines.

Below Right: 1997 Jeep Wrangler Sahara. The Sahara is a new addition to the Jeep Wrangler line-up in addition to the existing SE and Sport versions.

Bottom Right: 1997 Jeep Wrangler Sport. The Jeep Wrangler remains the 'icon' of the brand, offering open-top fun with legendary off-road capability to first-time sport-utility buyers as well as seasoned off-highway enthusiasts.

Left and Below Left: 1997 Jeep Cherokee SE. The Cherokee is the original four-door compact sport-utility vehicle. It continues to offer buyers one of the best-performing vehicles with all the traditional Jeep capabilities at an attainable price. The Jeep Cherokee line now includes the SE, Sport, Classic and Limited models.

Bottom Left: 1997 Ford Mustang. The Mustang name, for all its rich image and heritage as a performance car, now has another claim to fame: Mustang models equipped with 3.8-liter V6 and 4.6-liter SOHC V8 engines now qualify as Transitional Low Emission Vehicles (TLEV) in four states.

Above: 1997 Plymouth Prowler. Like the Dodge Viper, the Prowler started life as a show car but was so successful it was quickly put into limited production. Unashamedly harking back to the hot-rod era, the Prowler is guaranteed to turn heads on every corner.

Right: 1998 Chrysler Cirrus LXi. The Cirrus is the successor of the LeBaron saloon. It was launched as a prototype in January 1994 at the L.A. and Detroit Auto Shows to get the public accustomed to its cab-forward design, and launched soon after. Power comes from either 2.0-liter 16V or 2.5-liter 24V engines.

Left: Chrysler Concorde LXi. The Concorde was launched as a prototype in Detroit in January 1992 and was one of the new LH generation, with a longitudinal engine. A saloon car with front-wheel drive, it is produced in Ontario, Canada. The new version was introduced in 1997. Fitted with a 3.2-liter 24V engine, the Concorde has a maximum speed of 130mph.

Below Left: 1998 Chrysler Sebring Convertible. Based upon the Cirrus platform, the Sebring Convertible was launched in Fall 1995 to immediate critical acclaim. The combination of its smooth and elegant lines combined with lively performance made for showroom success. Maximum speed is 121mph for the 163hp V6 version.

Bottom Left: 1998 Chrysler Sebring Coupe. The Sebring two-door coupe has front-wheel drive and a transverse engine. Like the Cirrus, the Sebring is available with two engine sizes, 2.0-liter 16V and 2.5-liter 24V.

Right: The flagship 1998 Chevrolet Camaro Z28 Coupe looks mean and has all the performance to match, with 310hp available from its massive 5.7-liter V8 engine. With a top speed limited to 155 mph and 0-60mph acceleration in under six seconds, the Z28 keeps alive the muscle car tradition of the 1960s and 1970s.

Below Right: 1998 Chevrolet Camaro Z28 Convertible. An elegant and purposeful-looking convertible version of the Chevrolet Camaro was launched in Fall 1993, a little under a year after the Camaro Coupe was introduced. 1998 saw the introduction of the light alloy V8 engine.

Bottom Right: Chevrolet Camaro Convertible.

Left: 1998 Chevrolet Cavalier Z24 Coupe. Both coupe and convertible versions of the Cavalier are powered by GM's 2.4-liter 16V 152hp four-cylinder in-line engines. Top speed is 118mph with acceleration from 0-60mph in under eight seconds.

Below Left: Chevrolet Cavalier RS Coupe.

Bottom Left: 1998 Chevrolet Cavalier Z24 Sedan. The latest version of the Cavalier first appeared on the market in 1994, when the 2.3-liter Quad engine replaced the ageing 3.1-liter V6. Later, in 1996, the 2.3-liter four-cylinder unit was replaced by a 2.2-liter version producing 122hp.

Right: 1998 Chevrolet Corvette Coupe. Power from the latest version of the Chevrolet Corvette Coupe comes from a 5.7-liter V8 producing 345hp. It is transmitted to the rear wheels via either a six-speed sports manual transmission or a four-speed GM Hydra-Matic auto unit.

Below Right: 1998 Chevrolet Corvette family. Thirty-eight years after its original launch in 1953, the Chevrolet Corvette is still one of the world's best known sports cars. The fifth generation appeared in Detroit in 1997, with improved small-block V8 and a new chassis.

Bottom Right: 1998 Chevrolet Corvette interior.

Left and Below Left: 1998
Chevrolet Corvette
Convertible. The convertible
version of the latest generation Chevrolet Corvette was
brought out in 1998. Long,
low and sleek, it maintains a
tradition of all-American performance cars that stretches
right back to the 1950s.
Although today's Corvette is
thoroughly modern looking,
there are still elements of its
design that hark back to the
earlier years.

Bottom Left: 1998 Chevrolet
Corvette Hardtop. With a
top speed of over 170mph
and 0-60mph acceleration in
five seconds, the latest
Chevrolet Corvette remains
one of the world's true
performance cars.

Right: 1998 Chevrolet Corvette Coupe. Power from the latest version of the Chevrolet Corvette Coupe comes from a 5.7-liter V8 producing 345hp. It is transmitted to the rear wheels via either a six-speed sports manual transmission or a four-speed GM Hydra-Matic auto unit.

Below Right: 1998 Chevrolet Malibu. Launched in Detroit in 1996, the Chevrolet Malibu is an all-new front wheel drive sedan, powered either by a 2.4-liter four-cylinder in-line, or a 3.1-litre V6 engine. Power output is 152hp and 158hp respectively, with both versions returning remarkable similar performance figures.

Bottom Right: 1998 Chevrolet Malibu interior.

Left and Below Left: 1998 Chevrolet Lumina Monte Carlo. The Chevrolet Lumina range was originally launched in 1989 as a saloon and coupe. In 1994, the new edition coupe, the Monte Carlo, was introduced, fitted either with a 3.1-liter 162hp or a 3.8-liter 203hp engine.

Bottom Left: 1998 Chevrolet Prizm. The Prizm is a mid-range car based on the Japanese Toyota Corolla. It has a 1.8-liter 122hp engine and a maximum speed of 118mph. Until 1998 it was sold as a Geo, before becoming part of the Chevrolet range.

Right: 1998 Chevrolet Prizm interior.

Below Right and Bottom Right: 1998 Chevrolet Blazer - GMC Jimmy. The latest edition of the Chevrolet Blazer was launched in Detroit in 1994. Three- or five-door versions are available, fitted with either an automatic or five-speed manual transmission. Under the hood the Blazer has a 4.3-liter V6 engine producing 198 hp and providing a maximum speed of 112mph.

Below Left and Bottom Left: 1998 Chevrolet Venture. A four- or five-door Minivan, the Chevrolet Venture this latest version of GM's ever popular people carrier was launched in August 1996. It has front-wheel drive, a 3.4-liter V6 182hp engine and the option of a long or short wheelbase.

Right and Below Right: 1998 Buick Electra/Park Avenue. In 1996 the Park Avenue range was relaunched with modern and sleek new bodywork. Two versions are available, both powered by a 3.8-liter V6, but producing 208hp and 243hp respectively.

Bottom Right: The 1998 Buick Riviera was relaunched in 1993 with new and larger bodywork. It was also at that time that a new 228hp supercharged version appeared. The latest 1998 model is available either with a normally aspirated 3.8 V6 producing 208hp, or with the substantially more powerful 243hp Eaton supercharged motor.

Left: 1998 Buick LeSabre. The latest derivative of the elegant and imposing Buick LeSabre was launched in 1992, featuring a transverse engine driving the front wheels via an automatic transmission with overdrive. In 1996 its power was increased from the original 172hp and it now boasts a 3.8-liter V6 producing 208hp.

Below Left and Bottom Left: The 1998 Buick Regal, though only available with a 3.8 V6 engine, is available in two different versions. The Regal LS Sedan produces 197hp while the quicker GS version's V6 produces 243hp. In terms of performance, the LS has a top speed of 121mph while the GS reaches a maximum of 137mph.

Right and Below Right: 1998
Buick Regal GS Interior.

Bottom Right: 1998 Buick
Skylark. The sporty and
luxurious Buick Skylark, in its
final year in production in
1998, is now available only as
a four-door sedan, powered
by Buick's 3.1-liter V6 engine.
Standard transmission is GM's
Turbo-Hydra-Matic four-
speed unit.

Left and Below Left: 1998 Cadillac Seville. A luxury car with front-wheel drive and transverse engine, the Cadillac Seville prototype was first launched at the Detroit Auto Show in January 1991. In Fall 1992 the first Northstar STS 4.6-liter 32-valve V8-powered production Sevilles appeared in the showrooms. Two engine options are offered on the latest Cadillac Seville range, both based on Cadillac's 4.6-litre 32-valve V8. Power output is either 279hp or 305hp.

Bottom Left: 1998 Cadillac Seville ST. The ST is not only luxurious and comfortable: its performance would also put many so-called sports cars to shame. Its claimed maximum speed is 150mph and, according to the factory. its 0-60mph acceleration time is just 7.1 seconds.

Right: 1998 Cadillac DeVille. Based on the Eldorado, the Cadillac DeVille is a luxury saloon car with an extended wheel base. It was first launched in 1993 with a Northstar 4.9-liter V8 engine but this was replaced by the 4.6-liter 32-valve unit in 1996. The DeVille was further modified in 1997 with the addition of Stabilitrak.

Below Right: Cadillac DeVille facia.

Bottom Right: 1998 Cadillac Catera/LSE. Launched in Detroit in January 1994, the Cadillac Catera is a luxury saloon car based on the European Opel Omega sedan. It is fitted with a 3.0-liter V6 24-valve 203hp engine that provides a maximum speed of 124mph.

Left: 1998 Cadillac Eldorado. The latest version of the famous Eldorado appeared in Fall 1991 when the sleek coupe was launched with lengthened and more elegant bodywork. It shares its V8 engine with the Cadillac Seville and its performance is broadly similar.

Below Left: 1998 Cadillac Eldorado. Under the Eldorado's coupe bodyshape is a veritable arsenal of electronics designed to boost safety levels in all road conditions. In addition to anti-lock brakes, the latest versions are fitted with Cadillac's Stabilitrak traction control device.

Bottom Left: 1998 Oldsmobile Alero. Oldsmobile's 1999 Alero is firmly targeted at import-oriented buyers — people who have previously bought Japanese. Standard equipment list includes automatic transmission, air conditioning, four-wheel disc brakes with ABS, and power rack-and-pinion steering. A DOHC 2.4-liter four-cylinder and a 3.4-liter V6 engine deliver spirited performance.

Right: 1998 Oldsmobile Alero Coupe. The Alero is a car with personality. It is stylish and fun to drive, yet functional, reliable, comfortable and safe.

Below Right: Oldsmobile Alero Coupe interior.

Bottom Right: 1998 Oldsmobile Aurora. Oldsmobile's flagship sedan combines knock-'em-dead exterior design with superb road manners, making the Aurora one of the most charming sport sedans on the market. For 1998 the Aurora gained refinement in suspension systems, steering improvements, and enhanced emissions' controls.

Left: 1998 Oldsmobile Intrigue. The Intrigue, Oldsmobile's all new mid-size sedan offers one bodystyle, one powertrain, one seating configuration, design that's both elegant and functional, and a high level of standard equipment. It is designed to deliver a blend of ride, handling, performance, and upscale features superior to the best mid-size import sedans in the market.

Below Left: 1998 Oldsmobile LSS Sedan. LSS customers may choose between the 205hp normally aspirated 3800 V6 engine or the 240hp supercharged edition. Both are now equipped with a 4T65-E electronically controlled transaxle which automatically adapts to minor internal changes during the car's service life to deliver consistently smooth shifts.

Bottom Left: 1998 Chrysler 300M. Launched in January 1998, the Chrysler 300M is a new sporty and luxurious saloon, with front-wheel drive derived from the Concorde/LHS models.

Right: 1998 Chrysler 300M. The 300M made its first appearance at the 1997 Detroit Motor Show and has two engine options, 3.5-liter 257hp or 2.7-liter 203hp.

Below Right: Chrysler LHS. A luxurious saloon fitted with a 3.5-liter 24-valve engine producing 211hp, the Chrysler LHS has front-wheel drive and an automatic gear-box. The New Yorker/LHS prototype was exhibited in Detroit in January 1992. In terms of performance, its maximum speed is over 130mph.

Bottom Right: Chrysler LHS. Derived from the cab-forward styling of the Vision, the Chrysler LHS provides maximum interior space from a relatively compact exterior body dimensions.

Left and Below Left: 1998 Chrysler Town and Country The sleek Chrysler Town and Country is the latest version of the company's luxury minivan. It is fitted with a transverse engine and front-wheel drive. Two engine sizes are available, 3.3-liter 160hp and 3.8-liter V6 183hp.

Bottom Left: 1999 Dodge Avenger. Though little changed, the 1999 Dodge Avenger is now fitted with 'Next-Generation' driver and front passenger air bags and is available with new exterior colors: Plum and Shark Blue.

Right: 1999 Dodge Stratus ES. For 1999 model year, the Stratus gets revised suspension to improve ride comfort, other modifications to reduce noise and vibrations in the passenger cabin, and the availability of a 2.4-liter Low Emission Vehicle (LEV) engine.

Below Right: 1999 Dodge Intrepid ES. While changes to the Dodge Intrepid are confined to minor trim and color scheme options for 1999, one important new development is the adoption of the Sentry Key theft-deterrent system now added to the vehicle theft security alarm.

Bottom Right: 1999 Dodge Durango 4x2 SLT. Dodge's Durango range is extended for 1999 to include the option of a 3.9-liter V6 engine in addition to the existing 5.2- and 5.9-liter V8 LEV engines.

Left: 1999 Dodge Caravan ES. For those requiring space and the highest levels of comfort, the new Grand Caravan ES Model gains premium leather seating, eight-way electric power seats, electric seat heaters, steering wheel radio controls and other luxury options.

Below Left: 1999 Dodge Electric minivan. GM's zero emission EPIC electric minivan is available in the Plymouth Voyager and Dodge Caravan models. They are now equipped with new nickel-metal hydride batteries for 1999, which increase the driving range more than 33%.

Bottom Left: 1999 Dodge Ram 1500 Sport. For 1999, four-wheel anti-lock brakes became standard on Dodge Ram 3500 Models while all versions gained upgraded sport appearance front bumper and fascia, grille, quad headlamps, fog lamps and graphics.

Right and Below Right: The 1999 Jeep Grand Cherokee marks a significant step forward for the brand. At launch, it could boast an all-new exterior and interior design, all new 4.7-liter V8 engine, all new multi-speed automatic transmission and all new 'Quadra-Drive' four-wheel drive system.

Bottom Right: 1999 Plymouth Prowler. The stunning retro Prowler was never intended to have the performance of a supercar such as the Dodge Viper. The Prowler, like the hot rods of the 1950s that provided its inspiration, is a car to see and be seen in.

Left: 1999 Plymouth Prowler. For 1999 model year the Prowler gains a new 3.5-liter SOHC 24-valve SMPI V-6 engine and three eye-catching new exterior colors: Prowler Yellow, Prowler Black, and Prowler Red.

Below Left: 1999 Saturn SLI. Both variants of the 1.9-liter four-cylinder engine (single overhead camshaft and dual overhead camshaft) continue to provide high levels of durability, performance and economy for the Saturn sedan models.

Bottom Left: 1999 Saturn SC2. Refined powertrain performance is the major Saturn SC coupe improvement for 1999. The result is decreased sound levels both inside and outside the vehicles.

Right: 1999 Saturn SWI. Saturn's wagons are intended to provide class-leading value, comfort and quality. They are marketed as 'affordable vehicle alternatives for today's practical lifestyles'.

Below Right: The Continental, Lincoln's four door luxury sedan, received a major makeover for 1999, with more than 400 enhancements. State-of-the-art semi-active shock absorbers, rear air springs, and new safety features are joined by the all-important optional hands-off cellular phone and automatic outside dimming mirror.

Bottom Right: The Navigator is a ground-breaking new addition to the luxury Lincoln range for 1999. A full-size sport utility vehicle, it has advanced load-leveling suspension and optional Control Trac for the smoothest ride possible, while the interior is as plush and comfortable as Lincoln customers have come to expect.

Left: The Navigator interior.

Below Left and Bottom Left: The Town Car, Lincoln's flagship, got a substantial makeover for 1998. As well as upgrades on the suspension, chassis and brakes, it has all-new exterior and interior designs. A first for the Town Car is an optional touring package offering more power and a firmer ride.

Right and Below Right: The Mercury Cougar is Ford's latest coupe, based on the Mondeo model but featuring a smart and sleek new two-door body. Launched at the 1998 Detroit Auto Show, it is available with 2.0-liter 126hp and 2.5-liter V6 173hp engine options.

Bottom Right: The 1998 Mercury Grand Marquis was significantly refined and updated to give it a more millennial look and feel. And to give the performance of the Marquis an edge over other full-size, rear-wheel drive cars, both GS and LS editions enjoy SOHC 4.6-liter V8 engines.

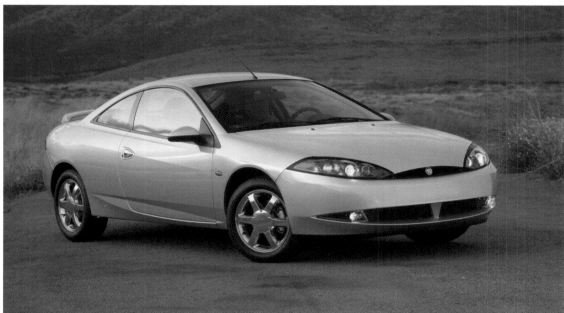

Left: 1998 Mercury Mountaineer. Mercury gave the Mountaineer elegant new styling with tone-on-tone paint and chrome wheels, and an improved new power train for 1998. V6 models are now fitted with Control Trac, while 5.0-liter V8 models are now available with a four-speed automatic transmission, with or without all-wheel drive.

Below Left: The 1998 edition of the Mercury Mystique got a makeover, as well as power train and chassis refinements. American design and European driving dynamics have been combined in the new manual-transaxle shift linkage which is aimed at pleasing driving enthusiasts.

Bottom Left: 1998 Mercury Mystique interior.

Right: 1998 Mercury Sable
Mercury made the Sable
better value than ever in
1998, adding more standard
equipment and updating its
design. Powertrain revisions
included a standard 3.0-litre
Vulcan V6 and a 200 hp
Duratec V6.

Below Right: 1998 Tracer LS.
For 1998, Mercury improved
the Tracer's four-speed automatic transaxle to give it
smoother shifting and better
response. One of the first
vehicles to receive a low
emissions' certificate, it
still has good all round
driveability.

Bottom Right: 1998 Mercury
Villager. Mercury's stylish
minivan was made over for
1998, and given new color
options, including the Gold
Sport Appearance Package.
Safety features include dual
air bags, side intrusion beams,
and optional anti-lock brakes
for this seven-seater vehicle.

Left: The 1998 Ford Escort LX.

Below Left: 1998 Mercury Villager dashboard and facia.

Bottom Left: 1998 Ford Contour SE. The fully equipped Ford Contour SE series is available with new Sport and Comfort options. 1998 also saw upgrades to the powertrain, chassis and interior features. Noise and vibration from the 2.0-liter Zetec engine has been substantially reduced.

Right: The rear of the Ford Contour SE.

Below Right: The 1998 Ford Mustang's 3.8-liter V6 and 4.0-liter V8 engines both complied with the tightest emissions standards, with fuel vapor losses also reduced. Added standard equipment and a drop in prices meant the Mustang was better value than ever.

Bottom Right: 1998 Ford Taurus SE interior fascia.

Left, Below Left, and Bottom Left: 1998 Ford Crown Victoria. Ford's full size, rear-wheel drive, V8 Crown Victoria enjoyed revisions to its front and rear suspension to match its contemporary design. Its 1998 chassis overhaul also included brake upgrades and added anti-theft equipment as standard.

Right and Below Right: 1998 Ford Explorer Sport. Ford gave its Explorer a new tailgate in 1998, improving appearance and cargo hold access. Added seat padding enhances comfort, with a new CD/cassette player improving entertainment.

Bottom Right: 1998 Ford Expedition. Ford's nine-seater Expedition rewrote the full size sport utility vehicle book. It has an 8,000lb maximum trailer towing capacity, meets Ford's ambitious ride and handling targets and still fits in a normal garage.

Left: 1998 Ford Expedition
fascia.

Below Left and Bottom Left:
1998 Ford F-150. Ford
celebrated F-150's 50th
anniversary in 1998. Its
streamlined exterior hides
either a split-port-induction
V6 or a SOHC V8 engine,
as well as revised front
suspension.

Right, Below Right, and Bottom Right: 1998 Ford Windstar. 1998 saw a new front fascia for Ford's Windstar minivan. Safety improvements included expanded availability of traction control and additional head restraints. Its 3.8-liter engines are claimed to be the most powerful minivan engines on the market.

Left, Below Left, and Bottom Left: 1998 Ford Ranger XLT. The Ford Ranger, America's best-selling pick-up truck, got new interior and exterior designs in 1998, with an electric Ranger also added to the line. A new Pulse Vacuum Hublock device helps switch between two- and four-wheel drive.

Concept Cars and the Future

Below: Ford GT-90. One of the most eye-catching concept cars of the mid-1990s was Ford's GT-90, first shown at the 1995 Detroit Auto Show. It was an early example of Ford's 'edge' look, with sharp lines and geometric design motifs.

The USA celebrated its centenary in 1996, exactly 100 years after Frank and Charles Duryea started the North American motor industry by 'mass producing' 13 cars in Springfield, Mass. during 1886.

Between then and around the time of World War II, America's motor industry lead the world in terms of sheer volume and also in terms of changing the western economies to the consumer-driven markets that are taken for granted today.

Post-war, even the massive US market reached something approaching saturation point, and as year on year growth could no longer be relied upon, so change and some form of rationalization of the industry became inevitable. Many makes and manufacturers disappeared, the majority to be taken over and absorbed into what became the 'Big Three' — General Motors, Ford, and Chrysler.

But not even rationalization on this scale could prevent others from looking enviously at what still remained an enormous and vibrant car market. First the Europeans, then the Japanese, and later still the Koreans all tried — with greater or lesser success — to get a toehold in the US market.

As we now know, the Japanese were the most successful of all and in one year in the early 1990s the Honda Accord actually became the biggest selling car in the States.

That was a shock to the domestic auto makers, but one thing is clear: they

are not taking all this competition lying down. And one area where it is possible to see exactly how hard the US auto manufacturers are struggling to meet consumer demand in future years can be seen in the vibrancy and imagination of their recent concept cars.

In the distant past, the nearest thing to a concept car was the prototype — effectively the first car off the line. But during the 1930s a Detroit components company called Briggs Motor Bodies revealed an aerodynamic-looking new sedan design with a Ford V8 engine under the hood. That car never made it into production, but the idea of the concept car took off, with Buick unveiling its Y-Job sports concept in 1939. So great was the attention the Y-Job received that GM adopted the concept car as an integral part of its marketing activities, producing a whole host of outlandish designs over the years which were displayed at GM's private Motorama traveling motor shows.

Most extreme of all was probably GM's XP-21 Firebird, a 370hp gas-turbine design whose appearance was based on the Douglas Skyray jet fighter.

In the more recent past, concept cars tended to be wheeled out at auto shows to attract attention and little else. Very often they were just an egotistical excuse for designers to let their imaginations run riot. And very rarely were they real cars in the sense that they had engines that could be fired up, suspension systems that operated, and even wheels that turned.

But today, the concept car plays a real and valuable role in assessing customer taste. If the public is enthusiastic about a particular design — no matter how outlandish it may appear — then it is very likely that it will find its way into production in the very near future.

Perhaps the best recent examples are the Dodge Viper and the Plymouth Prowler. The Viper was Chrysler's idea of a modern sports car, but one looking

Above: Ford GT-90. Powering the Ford GT-90 is a massive four-turbo 720hp V12 engine fitted midships. Ford's intention was to produce the fastest accelerating supercar in the world and it promised at the time to consider limited production of the car. In the event, nothing was to come of the GT-90.

back to the glorious days of the American Muscle car, when sheer brute power was more important than air conditioning and other modern day creature comforts.

Into a sleek, low, bright red body they shoehorned a massive 8.0-litre V10 truck engine and then revealed it at the Detroit Auto Show. The Viper was never really intended for production but the response of the American car buying public — perhaps in a reaction against the emphasis of recent years on emissions, fuel economy, safety, and other politically correct aspects of motoring that took all the fun and excitement out of the modern day car — was quite simply overwhelming.

As a result, Chrysler executives

looked around to see how the Viper might be built economically, bearing in mind that the volumes would never be great. Eventually they found a corner of a disused factory in downtown Detroit and put together a team of enthusiasts whose job it was to work together to bring the project to fruition. This team working in itself was a minor revolution as Detroit's auto industry had always worked with specialists in different departments doing their own thing and rarely having any day to day contact with specialists in other departments.

And so, for the Viper, instead of a designer designing a body and an engineer designing a suspension system and another engineer working on the engine installation and then later the suspension engineer trying to argue with the designer about where the pick-up points should be, and the engine guy arguing with the suspension guy because the

alternator was where the front strut had been positioned, they all worked together from day one to create a single design.

The result was a revelation. Not only could the Viper be built in limited production and still make money, but it was brought to the market in shorter time than any previous Chrysler vehicle. .

Exactly the same process applied with the later Plymouth Prowler. This extreme retro hot-rod was again unveiled at the Detroit Auto Show and again caused a public storm. In many ways, the Prowler at first glance looked an even less likely candidate for production than the Viper had. But the public loved it, and again Chrysler was able to put together a team that could bring the Prowler to market at a price that still allowed the company to make money. Perfect consumer economics.

In future years, as we move into the

next millennium, there will be enormous change in the sort of autos we all drive. And there will be change in the way we buy them because it is very likely that in part at least, massive and expensive glossy showrooms will give way to virtual showrooms courtesy of the Internet.

In terms of technology, it is likely that there will be more electric cars as battery technology is improved, more hybrid cars to provide greater range and acceptable performance levels, and maybe even cars burning new synthetic low-emissions fuels.

Perhaps most important of all will be progress in terms of IT systems — satellite-based monitoring systems that control traffic flows to avoid congestion and gridlock. Perhaps even accidents will be eradicated by the adoption of radar-sensing devices on every car linked directly to the brakes and engine management systems to automatically take evasive action with no input from the driver required.

Maybe the dream of fully automated road systems will one day become a reality, where you join a traffic flow, tap in your destination on the on-board

computer, and you will then be taken automatically to where you want to go, with all control of the vehicle taken over by the comprehensive traffic management system.

But even if just a part of this comes to reality, one thing will not change — and that is the American love affair with the car. Personal transport may be different in the future, but the auto will never be like a refrigerator — just another consumer item.

The auto manufacturers will still be striving to provide the sort of personal mobility that consumers want — in spite of increasingly onerous legislation in terms of safety, economy, and emissions.

That is why the concept car remains all-important in the auto business. It is a showcase of the company's talents and it is a means of creating excitement and interest in ideas and technologies, but most critical of all, it is the consumers' opportunity to tell the auto makers what they want to drive in the coming years.

A thumbs up from enough potential buyers is all it takes to bring a dream into reality.

Above: Ford's Triton concept takes the company into Dodge Ram territory. Most of the Triton is essentially the latest version of the all-successful Ford F150 pick-up, but it was restyled for this 1995 concept to look larger and even more purposeful on the road.

Left: Dodge Intrepid ESX. When it was first shown at the Detroit Auto Show in January 1996, the Dodge's Intrepid ESX was intended to give a very clear idea of the way in which the marque was moving in design terms in the years leading up to the millennium. The aluminum-bodied ESX was powered by a radical diesel-electric hybrid engine.

Right: Dodge Ram T-Rex. This huge six-wheel pick-up, the Dodge Ram T-Rex, is designed not only to carry heavy loads, but also to intimidate all other drivers on the road. Its intention was to out-tow, out-off-road, out-maneuver, out-haul, and out-run anything in its class.

Above: Chrysler's LHX, unveiled alongside the Dodge Intrepid ESX at the 1996 Detroit Auto Show, looks sleek and practical and suggests that a family sedan need not look dull and uninteresting. But it is inevitable that any production model based on this design would have to have a taller cabin — a roofline like this is strictly for show.

Right and Opposite Page, Top: The 1997 Dodge Dakota Sidewinder concept truck combines the Dodge Viper GTS-R's monstrous 600-plus horsepower engine with a Trans Am-based chassis and design cues from the great pickup trucks of yesterday and today.

426

Left: EVI. General Motors is the first major automaker in modern times to market specifically designed electric vehicles to the public.

Right, Below Right, and Bottom Right: The two-seat EV1 — the first vehicle in the company's history to carry a GM designation — went on sale in four western markets of Los Angeles, San Diego, Phoenix, and Tucson in December 1996.

Above: EV1 Parallel Hybrid. GM continues to investigate possible alternative fuel sources for volume cars. Having launched a fully electric version of the EV1, it then took the same body concept and fitted a parallel hybrid power source, providing the range of a conventional internal combustion engine, with the environmentally friendliness of electric motors.

Left: The SHO-Star was another look by Ford's designers and engineers at the mini-van concept, which, though it looked quite attractive, did relatively little to advance the cause of improved packaging.

Below Left: Turing Ka. Buoyed by the success of the sub-compact Ka in Europe, Ford's designers made regular attempts to take the basic package and develop other possible variants. The Turing Ka, with its bright green bodywork accented in black, sought to attract an even younger audience.

Right: In the cabin of the Ford Turing Ka, the interior continued the young and brash theme with extensive use of body-colored metal and brightly designed fabrics.

Below Right, Bottom Right, and Far Right, Bottom: Mercury's Fusion was a chunky compact concept with a large glass area designed to provide maximum light and feeling of space to the interior. Its elegant two-door design hints at the appearance of future Ford compact models.

Left: Ford's Powerforce concept was a Triton 6.8-liter V10-powered super heavy duty truck that quite literally towered over other pick-ups. With its 8ft long cargo box, bull bars and power rotating running boards, it was indeed a unique proposition.

Right, Below Right, and Bottom Right: The Ford Indigo is nothing more than a race car for the road. It was inspired both by Ford's Formula One and Indy Car race experience. A 6.0-liter V12 engine powers the Indigo from 0-60mph in under 10 seconds and the car was rumored to pull 1.2g in corners. The Ford Indigo's body was designed first and foremost for aerodynamic efficiency. The front wing generates downforce and the rear wing produces still more. The radiators, which are positioned at the rear of the car, are cooled by air channeled along the car's flanks.

Left, Below Left, and Bottom Left: The Ford Synergy 2010 came about as a result of pressure on the auto manufacturers from President Clinton to produce a family car capable of 80mpg, and get it into production by 2004. This is an aluminum-bodied car for light weight and it is powered by a 1.0-liter direct injection turbo-diesel engine which operates as a generator driving electric motors at each wheel. Weighing 500kg less than a contemporary large car, the Ford Synergy 2010 also boasts a drag coefficient of just 0.2, thanks to its stretched tail and bizarre finned front wings. These fins also channel air along the sides of the car and house rear-view video cameras.

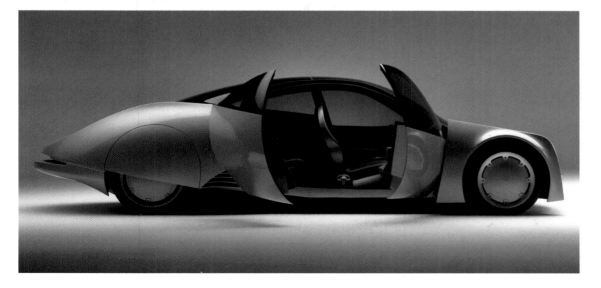

Right: Lincoln Sentinel. Apparently inspired by the famous French Facel Vega of the late 1950s, and retaining some vestiges of the appearance of the 1962 Continental model, the Lincoln Sentinel looks like a modern version of the sort of car Al Capone might have chosen. This is an extreme example of Ford's 'edge' design, and a very individual style.

Below Right: The Mercury MC4 was styled by the designer responsible for the Ford Indigo a year before — Mark Adams. The rear doors are back-hinged to make getting in and out easier and the rear trunk is a gullwing design allowing loading from the side. Inside cup holders are both heated and cooled, depending on the drink being carried.

Left, Below Left, and Far Left, Bottom: The Mercury MC2 was an early glimpse of what was to become the Mercury Cougar, a two-door speciality sports coupe based on the Mondeo/Contour/Mystique platform, and designed to offer fun, flair, and flexibility.

Bottom Left: Dodge Copperhead. Chrysler's sleek two-seater concept shown in 1997 is powered by a 220bhp 2.7-liter V6. With the wheels pushed out to the very corners of the car, the Copperhead looks mean and purposeful. In keeping with the Copperhead's name which derived from a poisonous snake, the interior is trimmed in snakeskin material and the tires even have a snakeskin tread design.

Right: Jeep Icon. The next generation of Jeep Wrangler will certainly be lighter, substantially more fuel-efficient, and more economical to manufacture than the current elderly design. In that case, it could well look rather like the Jeep Icon, a 1997 concept build on unitary construction principles rather than a body fixed to a separate chassis.

Below Right: Jeep Dakar. Essentially a four-door version of the Jeep Wrangler, the Dakar concept is longer than the production vehicles by some 380mm. Though designed as a concept vehicle, it is rumored that a version of the Dakar may find its way into production to compete with Japanese sport utilities that are already available in either two-door or four-door body styles.

Bottom Right: Chrysler's Phaeton concept looks back to the glorious and elegant days of motoring in the 1930s and 1940s. It's a four-door, four-seat convertible that features a separate windscreen to protect the rear passengers from the elements. Power comes from a 5.4-liter V12, essentially two of Chrysler's production 2.7-liter V6s joined together.

Left: Ford Alpe Limited. Hidden under the Ford Alpe Limited's SUV bodywork is the platform of a Mazda 626. That is because this is a design study for a joint venture between Ford and Mazda for a future SUV which both manufacturers would market in both two-wheel drive and four-wheel drive formats.

Below Left: Ford P2000. Though still at the concept stage when revealed at the 1998 Detroit Auto Show, the Ford P2000 will be on the market powered by fuel cell technology by the year 2004. Right now, there is a 1.2-liter ultra-efficient direct injection diesel under the hood.

Bottom Left: Chrysler Spyder. Early renderings of the Spyder concept reveal both the Karmann Ghia and the Porsche RSK influences. Crisp lines and simple full forms characterize this sports car design, which is distinguished by its strong wheel-to-body stance.

Right: Chrysler Spyder. Even in the design of the Spyder's 2.4-liter engine, Chrysler's designers did their best to provide a nostalgic appearance — in this case, a strong Art Deco influence in the intersecting forms.

Below Right: Plymouth Pronto Spyder. According to Chrysler, it ought to be possible to put the Plymouth Pronto Spyder into production and sell it for between $35,000 and $40,000. It is powered by a mid-mounted 2.4-liter supercharged four-cylinder engine producing 225bhp.

Bottom Right: Plymouth Pronto Spyder. Leather racing shell seats, tortoise-shell interior accents, a wrap-around windscreen, and special instrumentation are provided to give the Plymouth Spyder concept car a unique interior appearance.

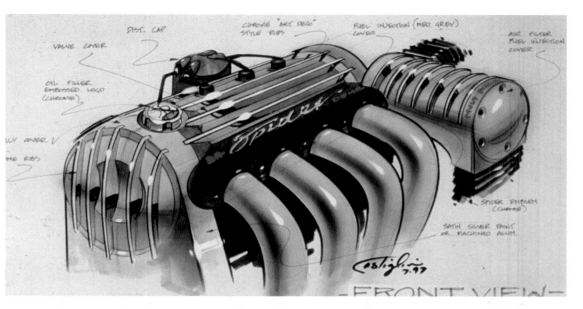

Left, Below Left, and Bottom Left: Chrysler Chronos. Strident and imposing, the Chrysler Chronos is yet another study into the luxury car of the future. 17ft 1in long, the Chronos is fitted with massive 21in wheels and is powered by the same V10 that is to be found under the hood of the Dodge Viper — though for the Chronos it is detuned to a more suitable 350hp. In terms of appearance, the Chrysler Chronos is perhaps an acquired taste. Chrysler's vice president of design, John Herlitz, has no such qualms, however. He says Chrysler has been seeking for many years the right look for a flagship model and with the Chronos they've 'hit the right chord.'

Above and Right: With the Jeep Jeepster, the designers asked themselves the question: what would you get if you crossed a four-wheel drive sport utility with a sports car? The Jeepster certainly looks the business, not least because of the red stripes on its tires, but whether anything of this nature will ever make it into production has to be considered unlikely. The Jeepster is a V8-powered, highly sophisticated off-road design with electronically adjustable suspension that allows the driver to raise the whole car some 4in when extra ground clearance is required.

Left, Below Left, Bottom Left, and Far Left, Bottom: The Chrysler Pronto Cruizer is a serious study of volume car design in the not too distant future. It hints at coming products not just for the US market, but for Europe and around the world too. The three-door Aztec yellow Pronto Cruizer displays all the extreme spirit of the Viper and the Prowler — two earlier concepts that made it into production. The Pronto Cruizer too could well see the light of day some time soon.

CONCEPTS

Right and Below Right: The Ford Libre, first shown at the 1998 Chicago Auto Show, is a fun-to-drive, four-passenger, quad-door concept based around a sporty convertible body design. The intention was to provides accommodation for four while retaining the slick appearance of a two-seat sports car.

Bottom Right: Ford Tremor. Essentially a restyle of the Ford Explorer, the Tremor uses a 4.6-liter V8 fitted with Yamaha five-valve per cylinder heads. This boosts power output to a massive 380hp. Traditional leaf spring suspension is rejected for independent rear suspension from the Ford Thunderbird. In terms of appearance, the Tremor is less brash than the production Explorer.

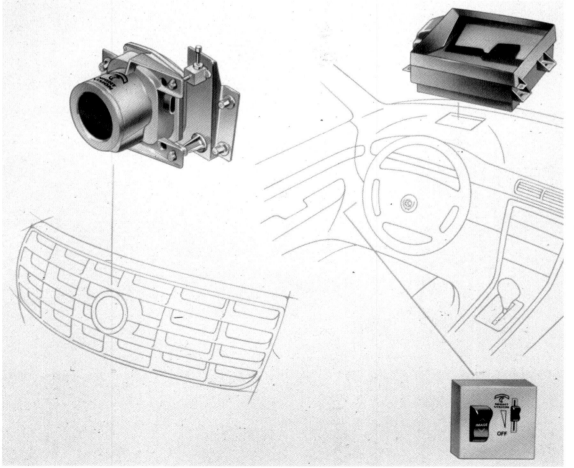

Above and Left: Cadillac Technology Night Vision. First shown on concept cars, Cadillac's advanced technology system — called Night Vision — uses infrared technology and a 'head-up display' to alert night-time drivers to potentially dangerous situations existing well beyond the range of headlamp visibility. Cadillac was the first manufacturer actually to put such a system into production, in 1998.

Right, Below Right, Bottom Right, and Far Right, Top: Buick's Signia, a concept multiple-activity vehicle first displayed at the North American International Auto Show in Detroit in 1998, is an exploration of ideas on how the family car of the future might look. It is based on the architecture of the Buick Park Avenue luxury sedan, yet also offers the versatility of a van or sport utility. The Signia takes as a starting point the idea that modern family life is packed with wide-ranging responsibil-ities and activities, and so its mission is to offer expanded versatility while maintaining the comfort, convenience, and safety provided in a current premium family sedan. Its most fundamental differences from a standard sedan are that it is notably taller, somewhat wider, and significantly shorter in overall length than the Buick Park Avenue upon which it is based. With an eye toward more efficient packaging, front and rear overhangs are aggressively trimmed to emphasize Signia passenger and cargo-carrying utility.

444

Below: Chrysler's CCV, or Composite Concept Vehicle, is a study in the use of new materials and cost-effective manufacturing techniques. Though the CCV is unlikely to win any beauty contents, its thermoplastic glass-reinforced composite structure and panels result in light weight and low manufacturing cost.

Index